FAST TRACK TO READING

Accelerated Learning for EFL and ESOL Students

Teacher's Book

Roger Scott
with Anna Phillips

With an Introduction by Peter Viney

Garnet
EDUCATION

Published by
Garnet Publishing Ltd.
8 Southern Court
South Street
Reading RG1 4QS, UK

ISBN: 978 1 85964 513 0

British Library Cataloguing-in-Publication Data
A catalogue record for this book is available from the British
Library.

Production
Project manager: Kate Brown
Pedagogical consultant: Anna Phillips
Editorial team: Kate Brown, Jenny Watson
Design: Mike Hinks
Layout: Christin Helen Auth, Sarah Church,
                          Bob House

Every effort has been made to trace the copyright holders,
and we apologize in advance for any unintentional
omissions. We will be happy to insert the appropriate
acknowledgements in any subsequent editions.

Printed and bound in Lebanon by International Press.

Contents

Consonant clusters

22	S T ~ ~ S T	/st/	58
23	C R T R	/kɾ/ /tɾ/	60
24	B R D R F R G R P R	/bɾ/ /dɾ/ /fɾ/ /gɾ/ /pɾ/	62

Vowel + consonant + vowel (lengthens first vowel)

25	A ~ E	/æ/ /eɪ/	64
26	I ~ E	/ɪ/ /aɪ/	66
27	O ~ E	/ɒ/ /əʊ/	68

The names of the letters

28	A B C D E	–	70

Consonant clusters

29	B L C L F L G L P L S L	/bl/ /kl/ /fl/ /gl/ /pl/ /sl/	72
30	~ N D ~ N K ~ N T ~ N C H	/nd/ /ŋk/ /nt/ /ntʃ/	74
31	S C S K S M S N S P S W	/sk/ /sm/ /sn/ /sp/ /sw/	76
32	~ N G	/ŋ/	78

Long vowels

33	O R O R E A W	/ɔː/	80
34	O W O U ~	/aʊ/	82
35	~ Y	/eɪ/ /aɪ/ /iː/ /i/	84
36	O Y ~ O I ~	/ɔɪ/	86
37	I R U R O R	/ɜː/	88

Soft *c*

38	~ C E C E ~ C I	/s/ /se/ /sɪ/	90

Vowels and their relation to consonants

Alternative vowel sounds for the same spelling

Silent consonants

The names of the letters

Introduction

By Peter Viney

What is it?

Fast Track to Reading is an accelerated reading programme designed for adult learners of English who are not readily able to read the Roman alphabet. It can be used for students who cannot read at all and for students who cannot cope with reading at speed.

It is **not** a course in English language teaching.

Who is it for?

Fast Track to Reading has been designed as a decoding or **code-cracking** programme, as explained below, in relation to the following groups of students.

1. **Literate students of linear languages**
   Adult learners of English who can read and write in another linear phonetic language (Arabic, Farsi and languages with Cyrillic script) have already mastered the concept of a linear system where symbols represent sounds. They need to crack the code of a written language which uses different symbols in a different direction. This can be done swiftly, in a programmed manner. A global reading element is added, as well as a pictorial element, to make the material feel relevant and interesting for adults.

2. **Literate students of pictographic languages**
   Adult learners who are conversant with pictographic languages, such as Mandarin or Cantonese, already have a concept of reading. They will almost certainly have some idea of phonetic representation as well, and will be familiar with Western numbers. They need more work than students of linear languages. The inclusion of a global reading element, designed to familiarize them with the shape (rather than the phonetic build-up) of the most frequent words, will help them.

3. **Illiterate students**
   This group will take longer, because the concept of reading also needs to be acquired, though the problem of interference from their own language is lessened. The programme has even been used with illiterate students from Roman alphabet cultures, and the latter parts will help native-speaker dyslexics.

It is **not** suitable for teaching initial reading skills to young children.

How is it integrated with other materials?

1. Groups of students who are totally unfamiliar with the English alphabet can use it as a pre-course, before starting a course where reading is an integral element of the course, i.e., the majority of current textbooks. It has been found that students give full energy and attention to the decoding in the programme, but the concentration is intense and 10–15 minutes is the maximum attention span. We suggest starting a lesson with 10–15 minutes' reading, going on to oral work with no written element, followed by ten minutes' writing practice, which starts with straight pattern practice. Then review the reading at speed for the last five minutes. Using this method, we can teach students to read effectively enough to join an ordinary beginner class in 56 fifty-minute lessons.

2. It can be used as a reading element in parallel with a simple starter-level course. Again, it would start and end a normal lesson. These students will be exposed to unprogrammed reading from the course book, but as the early words they encounter are so often irregular in spelling (or rather, follow less frequent rules), the two courses should be kept strictly separate.

3. Where there are some students unfamiliar with the English alphabet mixed in a class with others who are familiar with the English alphabet, this programme can be used for self-study outside class with the accompanying audio material. Its use should be demonstrated to them.

4. It can be used as a supplementary remedial element where students have supposedly 'learnt' the English alphabet, but are slow readers. They would be advised to move very quickly through the early (easier) units.

Method

The basic method might seem strange at first. When you teach children to read, you assume that they already know what a *dog, cat, hen, pen*, etc., is – recognizing both the sound and the picture. The new element is the written word. Where efforts to teach adults at speed break down is the assumption that they will also need to **understand** *pin, pot* and *pen* in order to decode the word. As a result, the teacher ends up trying to teach them a foreign language and a reading and writing system simultaneously. The result is massive overload.

In fact, adults get great satisfaction from learning to decode the sound/letter relationship at speed. You can largely sacrifice meaning, and focus on decoding. You can then use low-frequency words or, if necessary, use nonsense words (*sat/set/seat/sit/sot/sut*), though we have avoided this as much as possible in the book. You can also use words they may already know, like *Ali, Arab, Iraq, Basra*, etc. As travellers to countries with different reading and writing systems will attest, you can gain pleasure from simply looking at a sign and working out *Co-ca Co-la* in an unfamiliar code.

Although not immediately necessary, we introduce capitals simultaneously, because many more adults are using a computer keyboard nowadays.

However, the teacher will use the **sound** of the letter – as opposed to the **name** of the letter – whether they are in lower case or capitals. For example, the teacher will use the sound /æ/, rather than /eɪ/, to describe the letter a/A. This is obvious to any primary teacher, but in the USA particularly, there has been a persistent tendency to name the letters A /eɪ/, B /biː/, C /siː/ rather than to say a /æ/, b /b/, c /k/. It is difficult to say the consonants without a minimal semi-vowel sound, but teachers should persist in minimizing this. You need to get as close to b /b/, c /k/ (rather than b /bə/, c /kə/) as you can, although it is impossible to eliminate the vowel sound entirely. At a later point (Unit 28), the teacher will need to teach the names of the letters as used for spelling out loud.

The phonetics on the contents pages are vital. We have considered their use in the Course Book units, but when students are struggling to cope with 26 letters, experience has proven it counterproductive to expose them to 44 phonetic symbols as well. Teachers who are not fluent with phonetics will find that their gradual introduction will not cause them problems. As only one or two sounds are introduced at a time, the phonetic chart supplied on page 11 will enable the teacher to become familiar with the phonetics.

Does it recognize global reading?

The debate about teaching reading to children is split between believers in synthetic phonics at one extreme, and believers in global/whole-word reading at the other. For many years, the whole-word approach was dominant in British English education. Supporters believe that children read more quickly if they look at the whole shape of a word rather than its phonetic components. In recent years, this approach has been mixed with the systematic teaching of synthetic phonics. Even the most extreme supporters of synthetic phonics will agree that the most common words are read globally, as a word shape. This is how readers of pictographic languages operate, in any case. Native-speaker readers don't spell out the most frequent words (*the, you, do, so, does, their, for, out,* etc.), they read them as a whole, like a Chinese character. A number of these most frequent words are irregular or – more accurately – they follow minor spelling rules, rather than major ones.

This aspect of reading is combined with synthetic phonics by using realia: signs, notices and logos. Practice activities aid instant recognition of these whole-word shapes. After the first few units, the most frequent words are constantly recycled in a variety of fonts: printed, handwritten, print script and capital letters. A variety of fonts is vital so that students recognize letters in different forms. For example, the letter g can vary greatly according to the font used: g g g g g G G g G G.

How is it organized?

The programme begins with numbers. Though very few, if any, learners will be unfamiliar with English number shapes, it is necessary for them to learn the English words for numbers at an operational level. It's how material is identified for practice, and on the audio CDs. We do not write out the numbers as words.

It then progresses to one sound–one letter combinations, beginning with the base sounds of isolated letters. This takes us to Unit 13 (*k, ck*) and Unit 14, where *qu* appears. Next come the more common regular and irregular representations of sounds and groups of sounds. This includes work on vowels and diphthongs, and particular attention to consonant clusters, which present special difficulties for the non-Roman alphabet language groups. Work on vowels for a few units is alternated with work on consonants.

Word frequency is subservient to phonic clarity in selecting the example words. However, the more frequent words are highlighted as **key words**. Some words will be of very low frequency – remember you're teaching sound-letter correspondence, not meaning. Towards the end, some of the consonant clusters themselves will be of low frequency, but students need to be able to understand and work with combinations like ~*ngle* and *str*~. From Unit 30 on, **sight reading** is stressed by having words that have **not** appeared in the presentation in the practice exercises, but which follow the same form.

Does it teach meaning?

Broadly, no. In testing the material, two versions were used. One had pictures for some of the words (*pen, pan, pin*). The other didn't. The version where meaning was attached via pictures in the early stages was not as effective. Once meaning was attached to some of the letter combinations, students stopped focusing on decoding and wanted to know what all the words meant. It is difficult to avoid showing meaning with some early words like *pen*, but once you begin, you will end up explaining *pan, pin, pat, pet, pot*, etc. The programme will slow down and, most importantly, student focus will shift from logical decoding to meaning.

To make it appealing, a few words have been illustrated in each unit. Importantly, this gives students a few mental images to tie to the new graphemes (e.g., Unit 9: *bus, bed, sunset*).

After the first few units, words are highlighted in signs, and international words and logos are shown, so that meaning is tied to some of these words. Later, words are shown in blocks and groups, e.g., computer screens, mobile phone displays and diagrams, so that students can pick out individual words.

Can I change the sequence of units?

The sequencing is as broadly logical as possible, but in many cases it's an arbitrary choice of which order to present particular graphemes in. Each unit revises only sounds which have already been presented in combination with new sounds, so the effect, as in any synthetic phonics programme, is cumulative. Therefore, unless students are using it only for rapid revision, the material will work best when used in sequence.

Instructional language

All instructional language is for the teacher only, and appears in a separate column.

Stressed and unstressed sounds

In common with many schemes for teaching initial reading to native speakers, we don't use the /ə/ sound on the audio recordings, but present *a/A* as /æ/ as in *map*. When words are combined in phrases, some teachers may prefer to teach the indefinite article *a* as /ə/ rather than /æ/ (as in *map*), especially where students are false beginners or currently studying an additional course with speaking and listening. With complete beginner readers, we strongly recommend using the sound /æ/ (as in *map*) for the indefinite article. Some native speaker accents do this in any case, while others pronounce the indefinite article as /eɪ/ as in *say*.

While weak forms (such as *were* /wə/) are important in teaching speaking and listening, in this programme we assume that words will be pronounced in the strong form (*were* /wɜː/) where two possibilities exist. When *has, have, was* and *were* appear later, the stressed or strong sound is used, not the /ə/ sound. The English as a lingua franca (an international means of communication) movement has pointed out that while students need to recognize unstressed sounds in listening (indeed, it would be a bonus if they used them in speech), the vast majority of non-native speakers, including teachers, use the stronger sound in these examples, and in doing so they are clearer. The aim is not to sound like a native speaker but to sound clear and comprehensible to the largest number of people.

Audio CDs

The Course Book comes with 5 CDs of MP3 files. The track number and track length are given at the top of each transcript box in the notes for each unit. Track numbers are given after the CD number, e.g., *1.1* is CD 1, Track 1.

How do I use the activities in the classroom?

This will depend on whether your students are complete beginners or false beginners. In this section, we give some ideas for each activity type in the Course Book units. Using a variety of activities will help you cater for different learning needs and styles, in addition to increasing motivation.

Read and say

These activities come at the beginning of each unit. Their purpose is to **present** the new letters and words. They can be adapted in many ways, and the notes for each unit will give suggestions for adaptations. With complete beginners, you may want to do all the sections of letters and words. With faster students, you can miss some of the sections out.

Make sure students are reading from left to right in the early units of the course. You could also encourage students to follow the words as they listen by moving their finger along the line at the same time. Several of the activities below give opportunities for student-paced work and pairwork, thus reducing teacher-centredness.

1. **Listen and repeat**: Students look at the letters/words. Play the CD for the first section. Students listen to each sound and repeat. Check students are producing the correct sound. Replay, and repeat the procedure if necessary. Go on to the next section of letters/words and repeat the procedure, or use one of the other procedures below.
2. **Problem-solving**: Students 'have a go' at saying the sounds. Do not confirm or correct. Play the CD; students listen. Elicit the correct sound for each letter/word. You can do this using flashcards, an OHT of the page, or with the letters/words written on the board/interactive whiteboard (IWB). Practise the sounds using the CD, so that students listen and repeat.
3. **Listen and read**: Students listen to a section of sounds/words with their books open. Do not ask them to repeat at this stage. Replay the CD for that section two or three times. Then elicit the correct pronunciation for each sound/word.
4. **Further practice**: Say one of the sounds/words yourself. Students point to the correct sound/word. Once students have got the idea, it can be done as a pairwork activity, with one student saying the word and the other pointing. This is an effective activity for kinaesthetic students. Or tell students which section to look at. Say a number, then students tell you the corresponding sound/word. Alternatively, say a sound or word, and students tell you the number. Once students have got the idea, the activity can be done as pairwork.

Number the words

This is a student-centred activity which gives further practice in relating sight and sound of the new letters/words. All the words are on the CD, but you could read the words out yourself, if you prefer. Give students time to read through the words silently before you play the CD. The CD can be played just once for fast classes, or two or three times for weaker classes. There are more ideas in the notes in each unit for these activities.

Once students have filled in the numbers for each line of words, the activity can be exploited further, if you wish. Here are some ideas for games and pairwork:

1. **Pairwork:** Students read the words out to each other in the correct order. Student 1 (S1) reads odd-numbered words; Student 2 (S2) reads even-numbered words.
2. **Class work:** Go round the class with students saying one word each, in the correct order. (Choose students at random.)
3. **Spot the mistake:** Read the words out in the correct order, with the students following in their books. Say a different word at random. Students shout out 'wrong' when they hear it. (This is probably for faster classes only, but good fun if you can explain it!)

Listen and tick

The classroom technique of 'listen and tick' is an important one as it is used extensively in teaching and testing materials in EFL. It is a good technique because the output – the tick – is non-linguistic, so students can concentrate on listening, without worrying about speaking or writing.

It is another student-centred activity, but this time, students need to discriminate between words and sounds. As well as the new words for the unit, students review some of the previously learned words. Give students time to read all the words silently before you play the CD. Once again, you can vary the number of times you play the CD, depending on your students' ability.

1. **Pairwork:** S1 reads out the ticked word from the first pair of words. S2 reads out the unticked word. Continue with the remaining pairs of words.
2. **Listen and repeat:** Drill or practise the words in each pair.

Read, then listen and check

Rather than simply getting students to listen and repeat, this activity asks students to be more active and independent by working out for themselves the correct pronunciation of each word. In other words, students apply the spelling and pronunciation rules they have learned so far.

The CD is used for students to compare and check their pronunciation in a more student-centred way. Ideas for further practice include:

1. **Group work:** In groups of three or four, students take it in turns to read the list of words until they hesitate or stop. Which students can read the furthest without hesitation?
2. **Play and stop:** Play the CD then pause it at random. Students tell you what the next word should be.

Flashcard activities, games and pairwork

The flashcards are supplied on a CD with the Teacher's Book, to be printed off by the teacher. There are four flashcards per A4 page, with one word/letter on each card. The unit number can be found in the bottom right-hand corner of each card. You could also write the unit number on the back. An 'R' next to the unit number indicates words for revision. The flashcards can be printed double-sided.

All the letters and letter combinations covered, as well as the words from the Course Book Word List, are available as flashcards. You can use them to present, practise and/or revise the target language. The flashcards can be carefully selected to practise a target sound or letter combination, or they could be an almost random selection of words to revise.

The most obvious technique is to hold each card up so that all the class can see the letter/word and elicit the pronunciation, either chorally or individually. Use a maximum of 10–12 cards at any one time. When you have been through all the cards once, go through them again, at speed. Students can also test each other with a partner or in small groups. If you have a large class, you might need to make multiple copies of each flashcard in order to provide enough for all the groups to practise with.

Other flashcard activities and games are:
1. **Hide and say:** Use a blank piece of card to hide part of the word. Native speakers can identify a word from the tops of the letters only, and the first 2–3 letters of a word. This should be treated as a game, and you can gradually reveal the rest of the word until students can identify it.
2. **Point and say:** Attach the words to the board or a noticeboard in the room. Point to each word randomly and elicit the pronunciation. Students can also do this with a partner or in groups, with words spread out on the desk or table.
3. **Word sets:** Sets of flashcards can be shuffled. Then, with a partner, students can organize them into groups, for example, words beginning with the same letter, words containing the same sounds, etc.
4. **Card games:** One or two simple card games can be adapted for use with flashcards, for example, 'snap' or 'matching pairs'.

    In snap, partners or a small group of students have a set of flashcards each. Each student takes it in turns to place a card face up in front of him/her on the table. When another student places a card on the table containing the same word, the students shout *snap*. The first student to shout *snap* takes all the cards on the table. The game then continues. The winner of the game is the student with the most cards.

    For matching pairs, two sets of flashcards are placed face down and spread out on the table. Students take it in turns to turn over a pair of cards. If the cards have the same words, the student wins that pair of words and takes them. If the pair of words is different, they

are turned face down again. The idea is to find matching pairs of cards, so students have to remember what is written on each one. The winner is the student with the most pairs of cards.

5. **Right or wrong:** Show a flashcard of the word *big*, for example. Say the word *big*. Students say if this is correct or incorrect. Show another flashcard of a different word, for example *cap*. Say the word *cup*. Students tell you if this is correct or incorrect. Continue with more words, saying the words correctly or incorrectly at random.
6. **Dictation:** Make sure students' pens are down. Show a flashcard for a count of three. Remove the flashcard. Students write the word.

Writing activities

The vast majority of the writing activities in this course are at word level only. The objective is for consolidation of reading and spelling. We do not attempt to teach handwriting in the course, but some guidance is given in the notes for each unit, to help with legibility. It is useful to have a stock of lined paper for extending tracing and writing activities if students have difficulty. Students can copy a word several times along a line. See the handwriting lines on page 128, which can be photocopied. At this stage, we would expect students to print words, rather than use joined-up handwriting. The main writing activities are:
• trace and write
• read and label
• separate the words

The words in the writing activities can be practised orally first, then set as written work. Use the board to demonstrate the written activity. You will need to go over: writing on (or slightly above) the line; writing in a straight line; letters with ascenders (e.g., *l*, *t*) or descenders (e.g., *p*, *g*), note that *t* is a half ascender (compare the heights of: *e, l* and *t*); spaces between words (but NOT between letters in a word); lower-case letters (unless writing names, etc.).

Exploiting the visuals

The visuals have been carefully selected throughout the course for interest, relevance and authenticity. They make the page more appealing and reinforce and give meaning to some of the target words. The visuals also help motivate students because they demonstrate that the words they are learning can immediately be applied to the real world. For students who are visual learners, the photographs and other illustrations are of even more importance.

Always exploit the visual, which is usually labelled, by saying the word and getting students to repeat it. In the later units, or with faster students, you may be able to ask a few questions:
What can you see in the photo?
Where is this place / thing / sign / man?
Do you like this photo?
At the end of the unit, or after a few units, you can show all the visuals on an OHT/IWB or on a photocopied handout. Ask students to match the visuals with the target words.

Monitoring and giving feedback

In the notes for each lesson, we often suggest the teacher 'monitors' during a student-centred activity and then gives feedback. So, for example, during a pairwork activity, the teacher will go round the class and listen to as many students as possible in the time available. In this course, activities will be quite short, so you will need to monitor different students each time as you will not be able to get round everyone.

You monitor for three basic reasons:
- checking students are actually doing the right task
- assessing learning and performance
- managing the class

While you monitor, you can:
- give help if necessary (but don't spend too long with one student)
- make a note of the general language problems students are having
- make a note of what students are doing well
- encourage and praise students, especially weaker ones

When the activity is finished, always give feedback so that students are aware of the value of doing pair or group work. Feedback can consist of the following:
- explaining or demonstrating one or two general problems you noticed while you were monitoring, then giving further practice
- telling students (as a class, not individual students) what they did well

Particularly with students at this low level of English, it is always a good idea to finish feedback with praise and encouragement.

Using an OHT or IWB

There are many uses for these. In this course, we encourage their use for the following:
- setting and demonstrating activities
- the feedback stage of the activity
- further practice activities
- revision

Using the OHT/IWB for setting and feedback means you can clearly demonstrate, rather than using long explanations. The ideal method is to photocopy a Course Book activity onto a transparency. For further practice, you can select words from the unit, or several previously studied units, and put them onto an OHT/IWB. You can then, for example, point to a word and the students say it.

Key words

These activities are based on the most frequently used words in the English language. Therefore, it is essential that students learn to recognize them. Most of the words are grammatical and have little or no meaning on their own, for example: *the, in, get, him*.

False beginners may know the words in their spoken forms already. However, it is better not to try to teach the meanings of the words as part of this course. The course does not attempt to teach grammar or meaning, simply recognition.

Using the course for guided self-study

There are notes in each unit for setting work for guided self-study. Generally, the advice is as follows:

Before the self-study takes place:
- say the sounds of the new letters for the student
- tell the student which unit(s) and/or exercises to do
- tell the student how long to spend on each unit and/or exercise (not too long without a break)
- explain activities such as 'Listen and tick'
- tell the student he/she can replay the CD if necessary, and repeat exercises

After the self-study:
- go over the correct answers for activities such as 'Listen and tick', 'Number the words', and so on;
- point to some of the words in the activities and elicit correct pronunciation as a quick check;
- tell the student if he/she should repeat any exercises;
- give praise and encouragement!

For each student doing guided self-study, use a file card to keep a record. Write the student's name at the top of each file card. Make a note of the units (or letters and sounds) covered, and the date. This way, you can keep track of where each student is on the course.

Phonetic chart

For the teacher's reference only.

Vowels

iː	see	siː
i	happy	hæpi
ɪ	sit	sɪt
e	ten	ten
æ	hat	hæt
ɑː	father	fɑːðə(r)
ɒ	got	gɒt
ɔː	four	fɔː(r)
ʊ	foot	fʊt
u	situation	sɪtʃueɪʃn
uː	too	tuː

ʌ	cup	kʌp
ɜː	third	θɜːd
ə	about	əbaʊt
eɪ	day	deɪ
əʊ	go	gəʊ
aɪ	five	faɪv
aʊ	now	naʊ
ɔɪ	boy	bɔɪ
ɪə	near	nɪə(r)
eə	pair	peə(r)
ʊə	tourist	tʊərɪst

Consonants

p	pen	pen
b	bad	bæd
t	tea	tiː
d	did	dɪd
k	cat	kæt
g	got	gɒt
tʃ	chair	tʃeə(r)
dʒ	June	dʒuːn
f	five	faɪv
v	van	væn
θ	thank	θæŋk
ð	this	ðɪs

s	so	səʊ
z	zoo	zuː
ʃ	shoe	ʃuː
ʒ	television	telɪvɪʒn
h	had	hæd
m	man	mæn
n	no	nəʊ
ŋ	sing	sɪŋ
l	left	left
r	red	red
j	yes	jes
w	we	wiː

Demonstration: Try it out

To show how the book works, we have reproduced a section from the Course Book page for Unit 2, using symbols to represent the alphabet. Ask a colleague to read the sounds/words from Unit 2, Exercise 1 (page 9 in the Course Book) aloud while you follow the symbols below. In order to simulate how it would be for a non-Roman alphabet student, it would be better if you do not cross-check with the Course Book page.

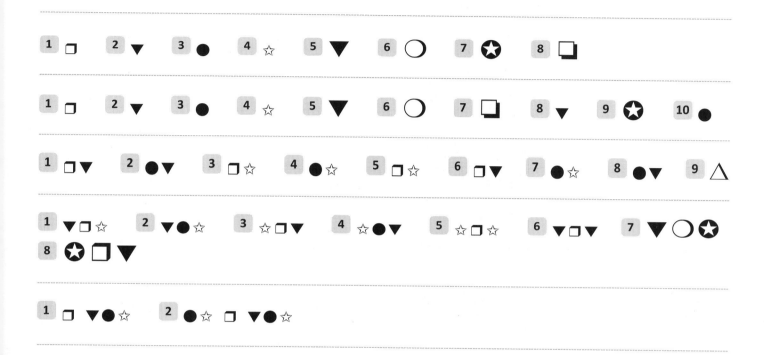

!	@	£	$	%	^	&	*	(	!	)
1	2	3	4	5	6	7	8	9	1	0

Objectives

By the end of the lesson, students should be able to:

- associate sight and sound of the numbers 0–10;
- write numbers 1–10;
- recognize the word *number* when it is spoken.

Adaptations

Faster/mixed-ability classes	Directed self-study
Go straight to Exercise 3.	As this is only the first lesson of the course, you will need to explain carefully what to do. If possible, monitor student(s) during self-study.

Note

This lesson is different from all the others in the course because it focuses purely on numbers, rather than letters or words. It could easily be missed out if you think your students know the numbers 1–10 well. Or you could do the lesson fairly quickly, then move on to Unit 2 straightaway.

Introduction

Spend a few minutes getting to know the names of your students and introducing yourself. Tell students that today's lesson is about numbers.

Exercise 1: Read and say

Exploit the visual of the calculator. Find out if any of the students can read the number in the window of the calculator correctly.

Focus students' attention on Exercise 1. Write the number *0* on the board. Elicit pronunciation. Use one of the following methods or a combination of the methods for each row:

- *Listen and repeat.* Play the CD one row at a time. Students listen and repeat each number.
- *Read and say.* With a partner, students take it in turns to read out each row of numbers to each other. Do not confirm or correct. Play the CD so that students can hear the correct sounds. Ask students to read the numbers again.
- *Pairwork:*
  - S1: (points to number 1)
  - S2: one
  - S1: (points to number 2)
  - S2: two

  Monitor, but do not confirm or correct at this stage. Play the CD for students to compare their answers.
- *Delayed oral production.* Students simply listen to the CD while following each row of numbers in their books. Replay the CD if you wish. Having listened to all the numbers, students move on to Exercise 2. This is especially good for East Asian and oriental students, who may be shy about speaking at first.

If students are complete beginners and/or are struggling, then give them some extra practice. Choose a different method from the list above to the one you used before, or use flashcards.

Methodology note

The number *0* is taught here with the same pronunciation as the letter *O* /əʊ/. If students give you the word *zero*, you can accept it as correct, but encourage them to use *O*. We have avoided the use of the word *nought* for this number.

In order to avoid confusion, we have also avoided the word *double* for two numbers, for example, 00 44. Students should say *oh, oh, four, four* and NOT *double oh, double four*.

Transcript ⏺ 1.1 (2 mins, 42 secs)

1 2 3 4 5 6 7 8 9 10
10 9 8 7 6 5 4 3 2 1
1 3 5 7 9
2 4 6 8 10
8 1 7 3 5 0 9 4 10 2 6
3 6 10 5 8 4 9 6 2 7 1
0 0 01 0123 010 0101 001

Exercise 2: Read the phone numbers, then listen and check

Use the telephone symbols to help you teach the phrase *phone number*. Ask students to read the four telephone numbers by saying the numbers quietly to themselves. Then play the CD with the students following the numbers.

> ### Methodology note
>
> In this activity, students are asked to deal with a simple but simulated authentic text. This shows students that what they are learning in this lesson can be applied immediately to the real world.

With a partner, students practise saying the phone numbers to each other. Monitor. With fast classes or students, you could get them to do the following pairwork activity (teach students how to say the names first):

S1: What's Ann's phone number?
S2: 0044 671 3289

Transcript 1.2 (0 mins, 51 secs)

0044 671 3289
001 516 8354
0039 218 5796
0084 796 3205

Exercise 3: Trace and write

Exploit the visual of the football shirt. Can students read the name? Encourage students to trace over the number seven with their fingers.

Now explain the task. First, students must trace over the grey numbers, then they should write each number in the space below. In other words, each number is written twice. Monitor and give help if necessary.

Closure

Use flashcards of numbers for further practice. Or write some simple sums on the board and elicit the answers, e.g., *2 + 2 = ?, 5 - 3 = ?, 10 - 10 = ?*.

2

Objectives

By the end of the lesson, students should be able to:

- associate sight and sound of the letters *a*, *t*, *i* and *n* as capitals and lower case in a variety of typefaces;
- recognize words containing the four target letters in a variety of typefaces;
- demonstrate understanding of previously learnt numbers 1–10;
- use classroom learning strategies for dealing with different exercise types;
- understand the phrases *capital letters* and *lower case*.

Adaptations

Faster/mixed-ability classes	Directed self-study
Exercise 1: start with the fourth section of words: *tan, tin, nat, nit, nan, tat, TIN, NAT*. If students have difficulty, go back to the first or second section.	As this is only the second lesson of the course, you will need to explain carefully what to do. If possible, monitor student(s) during self-study.

Words for revision
(also available as flashcards)

1   2   3   4   5   6   7   8   9   10

New letters/words for this lesson
(also available as flashcards)

A a /æ/   T t /t/   I i /ɪ/   N n /n/
an   at   @   in   it   nan   nat
nit   tan   tat   tin

Introduction

Spend a few minutes revising numbers 1–10, which were taught in Unit 1. Use flashcards or refer back to the visuals in Unit 1. Elicit the number of today's unit (2). Refer students to the visual of the @ key at the top of the Course Book page. Teach the word *at*.

Exercise 1: Read and say

Elicit/teach the sounds of the four letters *a*, *t*, *i* and *n* using the keyboard keys at the top of the Course Book page. Or you can write the letters on the board, or use flashcards. Make sure you elicit the sound of each letter and not the name, see the Introduction, page 7.

Elicit/teach the phrase *capital letters*. This phrase will be needed throughout the course; students only need to recognize it orally so don't write it on the board. Write the four capital letters on the board, if you haven't done so already, and elicit the sounds once more. Remember that you will be using the same sound for the capital and

lower-case letter. Write the equivalent lower-case letters on the board:
A = a   T = t   I = i   N = n

Point to the lower-case letters and elicit the sounds. Teach the phrase *lower case* if you wish, or you can use something like *small letters*. At this point, students are ready to do sections one and two of Exercise 1.

Methodology note

If your students are genuine non-alphabet beginners, you can do this activity one section at a time. Make sure students understand they should read from left to right! For zero reading ability, do some pattern practice in writing lines from left to right – e.g., zigzags, curves, loops – for a few minutes to get the students tuned into left-right movement. Thoroughly practise each line before going on to the next one. If your class are false beginners, you can combine the five sections into one longer activity. The suggestions for exploitation below are for a class of mainly non-alphabet beginners and so are quite thorough. If your class is more advanced, you can miss out some of the stages.

Focus students' attention on Exercise 1. You can use a combination of, or one of the following methods for each section:
- *Listen and repeat*. Play the CD. Students listen and repeat.
- *Read and say*. Use the numbers to elicit the sounds – either one at a time, or ask a student to have a go at reciting the whole section. Do not confirm or correct. Play the CD so students can hear the correct sounds. Ask students to read the letters again.

- *Pairwork*. With a partner, students say the sound of the letters/words to each other:
  - S1: Number 1
  - S2: a /æ/
  - S1: Number 2
  - S2: t /t/

  Monitor, but do not confirm or correct at this stage. Play the CD for students to compare their answers.
- *Delayed oral production*. Students simply listen to the CD while following each section of letters/words in their books. Replay the CD if you wish. Having listened to all the letters and words, students move on to Exercise 2. This is especially good for East Asian and oriental students, who may be shy about speaking at first.
- *Listen and point*. Tell students which section to look at. Say a letter/word at random from the section. Students point to the correct letter/word.

If students are complete beginners and/or are struggling, then give them some extra practice. Choose a different method from the list above to the one you used before, or use flashcards.

Students are now ready to try the third, fourth and fifth sections of the exercise. These are words rather than letters. Teach *word* but do not write it. Remember that the meanings of these words are not important at this stage; they are for relating sight and sound only, see the Introduction, page 8. Choose one of the three methods above for dealing with each section. Give further practice if necessary, again using one of the suggested procedures.

Transcript 🔊 **1.3** (2 mins, 4 secs)

1 a	2 t	3 i	4 n	5 T	6 I	7 N	8 A
1 a	2 t	3 i	4 n	5 T	6 I	7 A	8 t	9 N	10 i

1 at	2 it	3 an	4 in	5 an	6 at	7 in	8 it	9 @

1 tan	2 tin	3 nat	4 nit	5 nan	6 tat	7 TIN	8 NAT

1 a tin	2 in a tin

Exercise 2: Number from 1–8

Quickly run through the numbers 1–8. Students need to be able to recognize them and write them for this activity. Check students understand the task, then go through the examples. Play the CD. Students complete their answers individually, then compare them with a partner. Play the CD again if students had difficulty. Write the correct answers on the board so that students can self-check. The CD can be played a third time at this point, if you wish.

Answers

Transcript 🔊 **1.4** (0 mins, 32 secs)

1 an	2 @	3 it	4 in	5 tan	6 tat	7 tin	8 nit

Exercise 3: Listen and tick

Set the task and go through the example with the class. Play the CD. Students complete the task individually, then compare answers with a partner. Elicit correct answers. Play the CD once more.

Methodology note

When giving feedback for this activity, if necessary, copy the table of words onto the board (or use an OHT/IWB) and tick the correct answers. Some students may need to see an exact replica of what is in their book in order to understand fully which the correct answers are, and why.

Answers

Transcript 🔊 **1.5** (0 mins, 21 secs)

in	tin	tan	at

Exercise 4: Trace and write

Before you set the task, demonstrate the following on the board.
- The letter *t* is taller than the other letters.
- The dot on the letter *i* should be exactly above the 'stick'.
- Students should write on the line and writing should be in a straight line. (In Arabic, for example, a word can start high and finish lower.)

Students should trace the letters and words first and then write them underneath. Encourage them to say the words to themselves as they write. Monitor and give help where necessary.

Methodology note

This is an excellent activity for both kinaesthetic and read-write learners. The aim of this exercise is to engage these learners and to provide consolidation of word recognition, rather than teaching handwriting.

Exercise 5: Find the different word

This activity checks that students can recognize the target words in a variety of fonts. Set the task, preferably using an OHT/IWB to demonstrate. In the first row, *an* is circled as an example. Set a time limit of 10 seconds for completion (longer for weak classes). Students compare answers. Elicit answers, again using an OHT/IWB if possible.

Answers

at	(an)	At	@
tin	(tan)	*tin*	tin
it	it	(in)	IT

Closure

Use flashcards of some of the words from the lesson – see the Introduction for different methods. Tell students to read all the words again at home.

Objectives

By the end of the lesson, students should be able to:

- associate sight and sound of the letters *e* and *p* as capitals and lower case in a variety of typefaces;

- recognize words containing the two target letters in a variety of typefaces;

- demonstrate understanding of previously learnt numbers 1–10 and words;

- use classroom learning strategies for dealing with different exercise types;

- understand the word *vowel*.

Adaptations

Faster/mixed-ability classes	Directed self-study
Use flashcards of the letters and words in Exercise 1 in order to quickly check recognition. Then go straight to Exercise 2.	Go over the sounds for *e* and *p*. Make sure the students understand what to do. If possible, monitor student(s) during self-study.

Words for revision
(also available as flashcards)

A a /æ/   T t /t/   I i /ɪ/   N n /n/
an   at   @   in   it   nan   nat
nit   tan   tat   tin

New letters/words for this lesson
(also available as flashcards)

E e /e/   P p /p/
pan   pat   pen   pet   pin   pip   pit
tap   ten   tip

Introduction

Revise the letters *a*, *t*, *i* and *n* from the previous lesson, in capitals and lower case. Revise some of the words too. Use flashcards; if you have enough sets of flashcards, the revision can be done as a pairwork activity. You could also use an OHT/IWB to present letters and words. Point to each letter or word, then elicit the sound or word. Tell students that *A/a* and *I/i* are called *vowels*. There are five vowel letters in English; in today's lesson they will learn another one – *e*. Use the visual at the top of the page to teach the word *pen*.

Exercise 1: Read and say

Elicit/teach the sounds of the two letters *e* and *p* using the keyboard keys at the top of the page. Or you can write the letters on the board or use flashcards. Make sure you elicit the sound of each letter and not the name. Tell students that *e* is another vowel. On the board, write the three vowels that students now know: *a*, *e* and *i*. Say: *These are vowels.*

Revise the phrase *capital letters*. Write the two capital letters on the board if you haven't already done so and elicit the sounds once more. Write the equivalent lower-case letters:
E = e   P = p

Point to the lower-case letters and elicit the sounds. At this point, students are ready to do sections one and two of Exercise 1. Note that the second section practises both the new letters for this unit and the previously taught ones from Unit 2.

Focus students' attention on Exercise 1. You can use a combination of, or one of the following methods for each section:

- *Listen and repeat.* Play the CD. Students listen and repeat.
- *Read and say.* Use the numbers to elicit the sounds – either one at a time, or ask a student to have go at the whole section. Do not confirm or correct. Play the CD so students can hear the correct sounds. Ask students to try the letters again.
- *Pairwork.* With a partner, students say the sound of the letters/words to each other (e.g., second section):
    S1: Number 1
    S2: a /æ/
    S1: Number 2
    S2: p /p/
- *Delayed oral production.* Students simply listen to the CD while following each section of letters/words in their books. Replay the CD if you wish. Having listened to all the letters and words, students move on to Exercise 2. This is especially good for East Asian and oriental students, who may be shy about speaking at first. Monitor, but do not confirm or correct at this stage.

Play the CD for students to compare their answers.

- *Listen and point*. Tell students which section to look at. Say a letter/word at random from the section. Students point to the correct letter/word.

If students are complete beginners and/or are struggling, then give them some extra practice; choose a different method to the one you used before, or use flashcards.

Students are now ready to try the third and fourth sections of the exercise. These are words rather than letters. Revise the meaning of *word*. Remember that the meanings of these words are not important at this stage; they are for relating sight and sound only. Choose one of the three methods above for dealing with each section. Give further practice if necessary, again using one the suggested procedures above.

Methodology note

Net and *nip* are new words; students should be able to work out the correct pronunciation of the word because they have learnt the letters.

Transcript ● 1.6 (1 min, 30 secs)

1 e	**2** p	**3** E	**4** P						
1 a	**2** p	**3** i	**4** n	**5** e	**6** i	**7** t	**8** p	**9** e	**10** i
1 pat	**2** pen	**3** pet	**4** pan	**5** pin	**6** pit	**7** pip			
8 ten	**9** tap	**10** tip							
1 at	**2** pit	**3** net	**4** ten	**5** pat	**6** pet	**7** nit	**8** nip		

Exercise 2: Number from 1–10

Quickly revise the numbers 1–10. Students need to be able to recognize them and write them for this activity. Check students understand the task, then go through the examples. Play the CD. Students complete their answers individually, then compare them with a partner. Play the CD again if students had difficulty. Write the correct answers on the board so that students can self-check. The CD can be played a third time at this point, if you wish.

Answers

Transcript ● 1.7 (0 mins, 36 secs)

1 ten	**2** pit	**3** pin	**4** pet	**5** tap	**6** pan	**7** tip
8 pen	**9** pip	**10** pat				

Exercise 3: Listen and tick

Set the task and go through the example with the class. Play the CD. Students complete the task individually, then compare answers with a partner. Elicit correct answers. Play the CD once more.

Answers

Transcript ● 1.8 (0 mins, 17 secs)

pet	tin	pan	nit	tap

Exercise 4: Trace and write

Before you set the task, demonstrate the following on the board.
- The letter *t* has an ascender, i.e., it is taller than the other letters. (This is revision from Unit 2.)
- The 'stick' (descender) on the letter *p* goes below the line.
- Remind students that they should write on the line and writing should be in a straight line. (In Arabic, for example, a word can start high and finish lower.)

Students should trace the letters and words first, then write them underneath. Encourage them to say the words to themselves as they write. Monitor and give help where necessary.

Exercise 5: Read and label

Make sure students' pens are down; use the opportunity to revise the word *pen*. Ask students to look at the row of words (or use flashcards). Elicit the pronunciation of each word. Ask students to look at the row of pictures. Say the word for each picture. Now students write the correct word under each picture. Monitor and give help where necessary, not only with correct answers, but with handwriting issues. Write the words on the board in the correct order so that students can self-correct.

Methodology note

The pictures are here for consolidation and variety. Students do not need to learn the meanings of all the words. However, you could ask students to learn the meanings of the words *ten* and *pin* (as in *pin number*) as they are obviously extremely useful. *PIN* stands for *Personal Identification Number* and this is what people use when paying by credit card, instead of a signature.

Answers

1 tap   **2** ten   **3** pan   **4** net   **5** PIN #

Closure

Tell students to learn the meanings of the following words from today's lesson: *ten* (10), *PIN #* and *pen*.

4   M   D

Objectives

By the end of the lesson, students should be able to:

- associate sight and sound of the letters *m* and *d* as capitals and lower case in a variety of typefaces;
- recognize words containing the two target letters in a variety of typefaces;
- recognize numbers 11–15 in figures;
- demonstrate understanding of previously learnt numbers 1–10 and the sounds of letters *a*, *t*, *i*, *n*, *e* and *p*.

Adaptations

Faster/mixed-ability classes	Directed self-study
Use flashcards of the numbers, letters and words in Exercise 1 in order to quickly check recognition. Then go straight to Exercise 2.	Go over the sounds for *m* and *d*. Make sure the student(s) understand what to do. If possible, monitor student(s) during self-study. Tell them to repeat Exercise 1 several times.

Words for revision

(also available as flashcards)

A a /æ/   T t /t/   I i /ɪ/   N n /n/   E e /e/   P p /p/
1   2   3   4   5   6   7   8   9   10

New letters/words for this lesson

(also available as flashcards)

M m /m/   D d /d/   11   12   13   14   15
am   dad   dam   did   dim   din   mad
man   map   mat   men   met   pad

Introduction

Dictate the words *ten*, *pen* and *pin* from the previous lesson. Alternatively, use flashcards to revise the letters and words from the previous lessons. Revise the numbers 1–10, and the three vowels *a*, *e* and *i*.

Exercise 1: Read and say

Deal with the numbers first, before you go on to the other sections. Elicit how to say the numbers 11–15 in the first section. This will give you an idea of how well the students know, (or don't know!) the numbers. Go round the class in order, with each student reading out a number from 1–15 from the second section. Then play the CD for that section.

Ask students to listen only for the third and fourth sections. Then ask different students to read the numbers out again. If students need further practice, use flashcards, or write the numbers on the board. Point to the numbers to elicit the word.

Now refer students to the letters *m* and *d* at the top of the page and elicit/teach the pronunciation. Refer students to the *Men* visual and show how this word begins with the

letter *m*. Say the *m* sound as far as possible without a semi-vowel: *mmm*, not *m*/ə/. Focus students' attention on sections five, six and seven of Exercise 1. You can use a combination of, or one of the following methods for each section of letters and words:

- *Listen and repeat*. Play the CD. Students listen and repeat. Students can repeat in the pause after each letter/word. Or you can play two or three letters/words at a time and then ask students to repeat.
- *Read and say*. Use the numbers to elicit the sounds – either one at a time, or ask a student to have a go at the whole section. Do not confirm or correct. Play the CD so students can hear the correct sounds. Ask students to try the letters/words again.
- *Pairwork*. With a partner, students say the sound of the letters/words to each other, e.g., (third section):
  S1: Number 1
  S2: dam
  S1: Number 2
  S2: dad
  This activity helps students to revise numbers 1–14 as well as the words. Monitor, but do not confirm or correct at this stage. Play the CD for students to compare their answers.
- *Delayed oral production*. Students simply listen to the CD while following each section of letters/words in their books. Replay the CD if you wish.
- *Listen and point*. Tell students which section to look at. Say a word at random from the section. Students point to the correct letter/word.

Ask students to look at the words in section eight. If students' spoken ability in English is reasonable, or if you can use the students' native tongue, ask what is different about these words. Elicit that they are a mixture of capital and lower-case letters. Explain that this is because they are names. With a partner, students attempt to read the six names. Do not elicit at this stage. Play the CD for all six names. Elicit the names.

If students are complete beginners and/or are struggling, then give them some extra practice; choose a different method from the one you used before, or use flashcards.

Transcript 🔊 1.9 (2 mins, 49 secs)

11   12   13   14   15

1 2 3 4 5 6 7 8 9 10 11 12 13 14 15

2 4 6 8 10 12 14

1 3 5 7 9 11 13 15

1 m   **2** d   **3** M   **4** D

1 m   **2** d   **3** t   **4** p   **5** D   **6** a   **7** i   **8** n   **9** M   **10** e

1 dam   **2** dad   **3** did   **4** dim   **5** din   **6** dip   **7** mad   **8** man   **9** map   **10** men   **11** met   **12** mat   **13** am   **14** pad

1 Dan   **2** Nat   **3** Ned   **4** Pam   **5** Ted   **6** Tim

Exercise 2: Listen and tick

Exploit the visual and teach the word *map*. Set the task. Play the CD. Students complete their answers individually, then compare their answers with a partner. Play the CD again. Copy the table on to the board (or use an OHT/IWB) and elicit answers. Play the CD one more time if necessary.

Answers

Transcript 🔊 1.10 (0 mins, 20 secs)

man   map   did   pad   am

Exercise 3: Trace and write

Before you set the task, demonstrate the following on the board.
- The letter *d* is taller than the other letters.
- The 'stick' descender on the letter *p* goes below the line (revision).
- The difference between *m* and *n*.

Students should trace the letters and words first, then write them underneath. Encourage them to say the words to themselves as they write. Monitor and give help where necessary.

Exercise 4: Find the different word

This activity checks that students can recognize the target words in a variety of typefaces. Set the task, preferably using an OHT/IWB to demonstrate. Set a time limit of ten seconds for completion (longer for weak classes). Students compare answers. Elicit answers, again using an OHT/IWB if possible.

Answers

did	(dip)	did	did
man	MAN	man	(men)
am	(an)	am	am
met	(mat)	met	met

Closure

Students can probably already recognize the words *man* and *men* when listening or speaking. Without going into explanations about irregular plurals, etc., briefly explain that *man* = 1, and *men* = 2, 3, etc. Tell students to learn the spellings and meanings of the words *man*, *men* and *map* for a homework assignment.

5   o

Objectives

By the end of the lesson, students should be able to:

- associate sight and sound of the letter *o* as capital and lower case in a variety of typefaces;
- recognize words containing the target letter in a variety of typefaces;
- recognize numbers 16–19 in figures;
- demonstrate understanding of previously learnt numbers 1–15 and the sounds of the letters *a, t, i, n, e, p, m* and *d*.

Adaptations

Faster/mixed-ability classes	Directed self-study
Use flashcards of the numbers, letters and words in Exercise 1 in order to quickly check recognition. Then go straight to Exercise 2. See the notes for Exercise 7.	Go over the sound for *o*. Make sure the student(s) understand what to do, especially for Exercises 6–8, which are new activities. If possible, monitor student(s) during self-study. Tell them to repeat Exercise 1 twice.

Note

This is the first lesson spread over two pages. If you prefer, you can stop after the first page, where there is a natural break. Return to the second page another time.

Words for revision
(also available as flashcards)

Dan	den	dip	in	it	mad	map
mat	met	mid	Ned	pad	Pam	pan
pat	pen	pin	pit	tan	Ted	ten
Tim	tin	tip				

New letters/words for this lesson
(also available as flashcards)

O o /ɒ/	16	17	18	19		
dot	mod	mop	nod	not	on	pod
pop	pot	Tod	Tom	top		

Introduction

Use flashcards to revise the words *ten, pen, men, man, map* and *PIN*. Write these letters on the board: *a, e* and *i* and elicit that they are *vowels*. Tell students they will learn another vowel in today's lesson, the letter *o* /ɒ/. Write the letters *d, m, n, p* and *t* on the board. Tell students these are not vowels. They are *consonants*. Remember that the words *consonant* and *vowel* are only for spoken recognition at the moment. Do not worry if students are not fully clear about them at this stage; they will fall into place as the course continues.

Exercise 1: Read and say

Elicit/teach the sound for *o* /ɒ/. Use the visual to teach the word *dot*. For the first four sections of this exercise, follow the procedure from Unit 4, Exercise 1. Check throughout that students are using the short vowel sound /ɒ/ correctly.

When you get to the last section, ask students to find two names in the list of words. Elicit *Pam* and *Tom*. Remind students that we use capital letters for names. Try this new pairwork technique for this section: ask students to turn to their partner and read aloud 1 and 2. Do not confirm or correct. Play the CD for 1 and 2. Ask students if their pronunciation with their partner was correct or not. Replay the CD if necessary. Repeat for the next two words and so on, until all 18 words have been dealt with. If students need further practice, play the CD for all 18 words; students listen and read. Or, with a partner, Student 1 reads a number; Student 2 reads the word. Then reverse the roles.

Transcript ⏺ 1.11 (2 mins, 44 secs)

1 16   **2** 17   **3** 18   **4** 19

1 o   **2** O

1 o   **2** a   **3** e   **4** i   **5** o   **6** e   **7** a   **8** o   **9** i   **10** e
11 t   **12** d   **13** n   **14** m   **15** p   **16** i   **17** n   **18** a   **19** m

1 on   **2** dot   **3** not   **4** pot   **5** mod   **6** nod   **7** pod
8 mop   **9** pop   **10** top

1 in   **2** an   **3** on   **4** did   **5** not   **6** dot   **7** pot
8 pat   **9** pit   **10** pet   **11** tap   **12** top   **13** pod
14 Pam   **15** Tom   **16** mid   **17** mod   **18** mad

Exercise 2: Number from 1–7

Quickly revise the numbers 1–7. Students need to be able to recognize and write them for this activity. Check students understand the task and go through the example for the first row. Play the CD. Students complete their answers individually, then compare with a partner. Play the CD again if students had difficulty. Write the correct answers on the board so that students can self-check. The CD can be played a third time at this point, if you wish. Repeat the procedure for the second row. Note that in the second row, students have to number all the words, as the first word is not numbered as an example.

Answers

Transcript 1.12 (0 mins, 45 secs)

1 not	**2** top	**3** mod	**4** dot	**5** pot	**6** pop	**7** nod
1 an	**2** it	**3** on	**4** in	**5** pot	**6** pat	**7** pit

Exercise 3: Listen and tick

Exploit the visual and elicit the word *pot*. Set the task, which students should be familiar with by now. Play the CD. Students complete their answers individually, then compare with a partner. Replay the CD if you wish. Elicit answers.

Answers

Transcript 1.13 (0 mins, 18 secs)

pot	nod	Tom	Den	top

Exercise 4: Trace and write

Elicit the pronunciation of the words. Remind students of letters which are taller than the others (*d* and *t*), and the letter *p*, which goes below the line. Note that the ascenders on lower-case *t* and *d* are not as tall as an *l* ascender, or a capital letter. Set the task. Monitor while students are writing and make sure they are copying the spelling of the words correctly.

Exercise 5: Find the different word

This activity checks if students can recognize the target words in a variety of fonts. Set the task, preferably using an OHT/IWB to demonstrate. Set a time limit of ten seconds for completion (longer for weak classes). Students compare answers. Elicit answers, again using an OHT/IWB if possible. For extra practice, you can ask students to read out each line of words.

Answers

Exercise 6: Read and listen

Write the @ sign on the board and elicit what it means. Teach the phrase *e-mail address* using an example on the board. Set the task, and remind students once more about capital letters for names. Play the CD, twice if necessary, with students following in their books.

Transcript 1.14 (0 mins, 36 secs)

Pam at pop dot net
Tom at pen dot net
Dan at nat dot net
Ted 16 at top dot net
Tod 12 at map dot net
Tim 19 at pit dot net

Exercise 7: Read, then listen and check

With a partner, students practise reading the pairs of addresses aloud. This can be done one at a time with weaker classes. Then play the CD. Pause the CD, then go onto the next address. With faster classes, students try the first three addresses, then listen and check. Pause the CD, then students try the next three addresses. For further practice with faster classes, you can set up the following pairwork activity:

S1: What's Pam's email address?
S2: (It's) Pam at pop dot net.

Transcript 1.15 (0 mins, 28 secs)

Pam at pop dot net
Tom at pen dot net
Dan at nat dot net
Ted 16 at top dot net
Tod 12 at map dot net
Tim 19 at pit dot net

Exercise 8: Separate the words

This is new activity so it needs to be set carefully. Go over the example, preferably using an OHT/IWB. If necessary, show how words can be formed: *vowel + consonant* and *consonant + vowel + consonant*. If you think this is too difficult for your students, then they can just do the activity as word recognition practice. Students complete individually, then compare answers with a partner. Monitor and give help where necessary. Encourage students to copy out the words correctly. For feedback, ask different students to read out a line of words each. Write the words on the board for students to check. Do not erase – use for the Closure below.

Answers

pot / not / dot / pod / mop / top
dip / pin / pit / tip / tin / mid
ten / men / pen / den / met
pan / mad / tan / pad / mat

Closure

Use the answers on the board from Exercise 8 for further practice. Point to a word and elicit the pronunciation. Then number some of the words from 1–19: *1 at, 2 pen, 3 map, 4 ten, 5 not, 6 pot,* etc. Say a word – students tell you the corresponding number:

T: map
Ss: 3
T: pot
Ss: 6

Objectives

By the end of the lesson, students should be able to:

- associate sight and sound of the letters *g* and *v* as capitals and lower case in a variety of typefaces;

- recognize words containing the two target letters in a variety of typefaces;

- demonstrate understanding of previously learnt numbers 1–19;

- demonstrate recognition of previously learnt letters and words;

- recognize numbers 20–25.

Adaptations

Faster/mixed-ability classes	Directed self-study
There are suggestions for faster classes in the notes below for Exercise 1.	Go over the sounds for *g* and *v*. Tell student(s) which exercises to do. Remind them that they can replay the CD, or pause it, if they wish.

Words for revision
(also available as flashcards)

1–19	an	at	dam	Dan	did	dim
dot	in	it	man	map	men	met
mod	mop	nag	nat	net	nip	nod
not	on	pat	pen	pin	pit	pod
pot	ten	Tom	top			

New letters/words for this lesson
(also available as flashcards)

G g /g/	V v /v/	20	21	22	23	24	25
dig	dog	get	gig	God	got		nag
peg	pig	tag	van	vat	vet		vim

Introduction

Revise some of the words from the previous lesson. Introduce the letters g and v.

Exercise 1: Read and say

Faster classes: If you think your class probably knows the numbers, elicit the numbers 20–25, either using the book, or by writing the numbers on the board. Play the CD for the first section so that students can hear the correct pronunciation. Then students can practise and revise the numbers 1–25 with a partner:

    S1: (points to a number)
    S2: (says the number)

Weaker classes: If your class doesn't know the numbers very well, play the CD of the first section – twice if necessary – with students following in their books. Then ask individual students to read out a number. Play the CD of the numbers 1–25 with the students following in their books. Use flashcards or write the numbers on the board. Elicit pronunciation of each number randomly chosen.

Now focus students' attention on the rest of Exercise 1. For each section, you can use a combination of, or one of the methods listed in Unit 4. Monitor during the activities and check students are using the correct vowel sounds, as well as the target letters *g* and *v,* correctly. Remind students not to introduce a semi-vowel or schwa sound after the consonants, see the Introduction, page 8. Give further practice if necessary, using flashcards of the words.

When you get to the last section of this exercise, ask students to work with a partner. Ask them to say words 1–5 to each other. Play the CD of words 1–5. Now elicit the correct pronunciation for each word. Repeat the procedure with the next set of five words, and so on, until you get to the end. Replay the CD for all the words from 1–20. Give further practice; with a partner, students test each other on the words:

    S1: Number 5
    S2: got
    S1: Number 16
    S2: vet

Methodology note

In the latter part of this exercise, students make an educated guess at the pronunciation of each word before listening to the CD. It does not matter if students get the words wrong at this point. The key point is for them to attempt to work out the pronunciation independently using a problem-solving approach.

Transcript 🔊 1.16 (3 mins, 30 secs)

20　21　22　23　24　25

1 2 3 4 5 6 7 8 9 10 11 12 13 14 15 16 17 18 19 20 21 22 23 24 25

1 g　**2** g　**3** G　**4** v　**5** V

1 g　**2** v　**3** t　**4** d　**5** v　**6** m　**7** g　**8** p　**9** n
10 g　**11** v　**12** e　**13** i　**14** o　**15** a

1 dig　**2** dog　**3** get　**4** God　**5** got　**6** peg　**7** nag
8 tag　**9** van　**10** vat　**11** vet　**12** vim

1 dig　**2** did　**3** vim　**4** dog　**5** got　**6** God　**7** get
8 gig　**9** peg　**10** vat　**11** tan　**12** tag　**13** van
14 man　**15** met　**16** vet　**17** ten　**18** nag　**19** Dan
20 Tom

Exercise 2: Number from 1–11

Follow the usual procedure. For further practice, set pairwork: S1 reads out numbers 1–5 (S2 listens and checks); S2 reads out numbers 6–11 (S1 listens and checks).

Answers

Transcript 🔊 1.17 (0 mins, 38 secs)

1 dig　**2** got　**3** God　**4** vim　**5** peg　**6** tag　**7** dog
8 get　**9** vat　**10** van　**11** vet

Exercise 3: Listen and tick

Exploit the visual and elicit the word *dog*. Follow the usual procedure.

Answers

Transcript 🔊 1.18 (0 mins, 26 secs)

got　God　get　van　vim　gig　nab

Exercise 4: Trace and write

On the board, demonstrate the descender on the letter *g*. Then follow the usual procedure.

Exercise 5: Find the different word

Follow the usual procedure.

Answers

get	get	got	get
did	dig	did	did
van	nan	van	van
pet	vet	VET	vet
got	got	got	not

Exercise 6: Separate the words

This is only the second time students have done this activity, so it needs to be set carefully. Go over the example, preferably using an OHT/IWB. If necessary, show how words can be formed (do not write these words on the board straightaway, but demonstrate using example letters):

T: vowel + consonant [write *a* + *t* = *at*]
T: consonant + vowel + consonant [write *p* + *e* + *n* = *pen*]

If you think this is too difficult for your students, then they can just do the activity as word recognition practice.

Students complete individually, then compare answers with a partner. Monitor and give help where necessary. Encourage students to copy out the words correctly; it might be better to do this in a notebook or on a piece of paper so they have more space. For feedback, ask different students to read out a line of words each. Write the words on the board for students to check. Do not erase – use for the Closure below.

Answers

got / get / dog / peg / tag / dig / pig
van / vat / vet / vim
dog / dim / did / dot / dam
pod / pit / pen / pat / pig / pot / pin
ten / tan / tin / tag / top / tan
men / man / mop / mod / mat / map
not / nag / net / nod / nip / nap
in / on / am / an / it

Exercise 7: Read key words

Ask students to look at the lines of words. Elicit the similarity between lines two and four. (They are both in capital letters.) Set the task. With a partner, students take it in turns to read one word each from the first line. Play the CD for the first line. Elicit the correct pronunciation of each word. Repeat the procedure for lines 2–4. Play the CD for all four lines, with students following in their books. If you wish, you can do further practice of the words using flashcards.

Methodology note

These are examples of some of the most frequently used words in English. Most of them are *grammatical* words. It is very important that students can recognize them. Some students, whose spoken ability is ahead of their reading and writing skills, may already be familiar with these words. In this activity, the letter *a* appears as the indefinite article: *a pen, a map*, etc. When used as an article, *a* can have different pronunciations, depending on the speaker. We are continuing to use the /æ/ pronunciation to avoid confusing students.

Transcript 🔊 1.19 (1 min, 33 secs)

a　am　an　at　did　in　it　get　got　not　on
GET　IN　NOT　AM　DID　AT　GOT　ON　IT　A　AN
got　a　not　an　it　am　on　in　get　at　did
AM　NOT　AT　GET　ON　GOT　DID　A　IT　IN　AN

Closure

Use the answers on the board for Exercise 6 for further practice. Follow the procedure from the Closure for Unit 5. Focus on words with the two target letters *g* and *v*.

7   H   L

Objectives

By the end of the lesson, students should be able to:

- associate sight and sound of the letters *h* and *l* as capitals and lower case in a variety of typefaces;
- recognize words containing the two target letters in a variety of typefaces;
- demonstrate understanding of previously learnt numbers 1–25;
- demonstrate recognition of previously learnt letters and words.

Adaptations

Faster/mixed-ability classes	Directed self-study
Do Exercise 3 as a test. If students do well, continue with the rest of the lesson. If not, go back to Exercise 1. There are suggestions for faster classes in the notes for Exercise 8.	Go over the sounds for *h* and *l*. Tell student(s) which exercises to do. Remind them that they can replay the CD, or pause it, if they wish. Exercises 5 and 8 will need to be explained.

Words for revision
(also available as flashcards)

1–25   did   dim   got   mad   mat   ten
tip   top   van   vet

New letters/words for this lesson
(also available as flashcards)

H h /h/   L l /l/
had   hal   halal   hat   hen   hid   him
hit,   hop   hot   lap   let   lid   lip
log   lot

Introduction

Use flashcards to revise some of the words from the previous lesson. Introduce the letters *h* and *l*.

Exercise 1: Read and say

Exploit the visual and teach the word *hat*. Revise numbers 20–25 using flashcards, or write the numbers on the board and elicit by pointing to each one. Then follow the usual procedure for this activity, or see the notes on page 10 about how to use the activities in the classroom.

There are 25 words in the final section of this activity, so deal with five words at a time. Ask students to work with a partner. Ask them to say words 1–5 to each other. Play the CD for words 1–5. Now ask students to tell you the correct pronunciation for each word. Repeat the procedure with the next set of five words, and so on, until you get to the end. Replay the CD for all words from 1–25. For further practice: with a partner, students test each other on the words:

S1: Number 5
S2: let
S1: Number 21
S2: lit

Transcript ◎ 1.20 (3 mins, 15 secs)

1 h	**2** H	**3** l	**4** l	**5** L

1 h   **2** l   **3** v   **4** d   **5** p   **6** m   **7** g   **8** n   **9** t
10 i   **11** e   **12** a   **13** o   **14** L   **15** H   **16** M   **17** G
18 V   **19** T   **20** P   **21** D

1 had   **2** hat   **3** hen   **4** hid   **5** him   **6** hit   **7** hot
8 hop   **9** lap   **10** let   **11** lid   **12** lip   **13** log   **14** lot
15 hal   **16** halal

1 lot   **2** had   **3** log   **4** him   **5** let   **6** lip   **7** hot
8 hen   **9** lap   **10** hit   **11** lop   **12** hat   **13** hid
14 lid   **15** got   **16** van   **17** vet   **18** did   **19** top
20 lad   **21** lit   **22** mat   **23** hip   **24** hop   **25** tip

Exercise 2: Number from 1–7

Follow the usual procedure or see the notes on page 9.

Transcript ◎ 1.21 (0 mins, 48 secs)

1 lad   **2** lot   **3** let   **4** lap   **5** log   **6** lip   **7** lid

1 had   **2** hat   **3** hen   **4** hid   **5** him   **6** hit   **7** hot

Exercise 3: Listen and tick

This activity is a bit longer than usual, but you can follow the usual procedure.

Answers

let	lad	log	had	him
hit	ten	lad	lip	let

Exercise 4: Trace and write

Demonstrate the lower-case letters *h* and *l* on the board, and show how they are *tall* letters. Then follow the usual procedure.

Exercise 5: Read and label

Ask different students to read out the three phrases; correct their pronunciation, if necessary. With students' pens down, exploit each of the three pictures and elicit the target vocabulary. Set the task and check carefully that students understand what to do. Monitor while students are writing the labels. Use an OHT/IWB to give feedback. As well as giving the correct answers, focus on one or two handwriting areas, for example:
- leaving a space between each word
- tall letters – *l*, *t* and *h*
- letters which go below the line – *p*

Answers

1 a pot, a lid on top   **2** a laptop   **3** a hot tap

Exercise 6: Read, then listen and check

You can follow any of the procedures previously explained for this type of activity, or use the following procedure. Students read the six lines silently. Play the CD for all six lines, with the students following in their books. With a partner, students take it in turns to read a line each. Monitor and make a note of common errors. Give feedback and practise any words or phrases students struggled with. Play the CD once more.

a top	a lap	a laptop
a tap	a hot tap	
a pot	a hot pot a lid on top	a pot, a lid on top
a hot pot, a lid on top		
log	log on	log on a laptop
let	let him let him in	get him get him a laptop

Exercise 7: Read key words

Ask students to look at the lines of words. Elicit the similarity between lines two and four. (They are both in capital letters.) Set the task. With a partner, students take it in turns to read one word from the first line:
    S1: a
    S2: had
    S1: let
    S2: him
Play the CD for the first row. Ask students if they got any of

the words wrong. Elicit the correct pronunciation of each word. Repeat the procedure for lines 2–4. Play the CD for all four lines, with students following in their books. If you wish, you can do further practice of the words using flashcards.

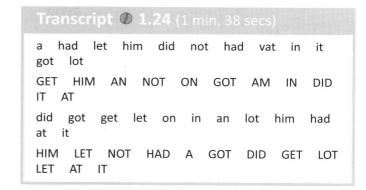

a	had	let	him	did	not	had	vat	in it
got	lot							
GET	HIM	AN	NOT	ON	GOT	AM	IN	DID
IT	AT							
did	got	get	let	on	in	an	lot	him had
at	it							
HIM	LET	NOT	HAD	A	GOT	DID	GET	LOT
LET	AT	IT						

Exercise 8: Find words from Units 6 and 7

Use an OHT/IWB to set the task. Make sure students understand they can only find words from left to right, or top-down.

Weaker classes: Write the words in the wordsearch as a list on the board. Students find the words.

Faster classes: When students have found a word and circled it, they must then write it in lower-case letters, for example, TAG = tag. Elicit answers using the OHT/IWB.

Answers

Closure

Use the wordsearch as the Closure.

8 U C

Objectives

By the end of the lesson, students should be able to:

- associate sight and sound of the letters *u* and *c* as capitals and lower case in a variety of typefaces;
- recognize words containing the two target letters in a variety of typefaces;
- demonstrate recognition of previously learnt letters and words.

Adaptations

Faster/mixed-ability classes	Directed self-study
Do Exercise 3 as a test. If students do well, continue with the rest of the lesson. If not, go back to Exercise 1. There are suggestions for faster classes in the notes below for Exercise 3.	Go over the sounds for *u* and *c*. Tell student(s) which exercises to do. Remind them that they can replay the CD, or pause it, if they wish. Exercise 6 will need to be explained.

Words for revision
(also available as flashcards)

cot   hog   hot   not   pop   tag

New letters/words for this lesson
(also available as flashcards)

U u /ʌ/   C c /k/

can	cap	cat	cog	cop	cot	cup
cut	gum	gun	hug	hut	mud	mug
nut	pop up	pup	tip up	top up	tug	up

Introduction

Show the visuals from Unit 7, Exercise 5 on an OHT/IWB. Elicit the phrases: *a pot, a laptop, a hot tap*. Ask students to write the three phrases. After a minute or so, write the three phrases on the board so students can check their spelling. Introduce the letters for today's lesson: *u* and *c*.

Exercise 1: Read and say

Follow the usual procedure, or see the notes on page 10.

Transcript 🔊 **1.25** (2 mins, 57 secs)

1 u   2 U   3 c   4 C

1 u   2 c   3 a   4 i   5 u   6 o   7 u   8 e   9 c
10 t   11 d   12 c   13 v   14 C   15 G   16 T   17 G
18 C   19 U   20 O

1 up   2 can   3 cap   4 cat   5 cog   6 cot   7 cup
8 cut   9 gum   10 gun   11 hug   12 hut   13 mud
14 mug   15 nut

1 pop   2 pup   3 can   4 cap   5 hog   6 hug   7 vat
8 cat   9 gum   10 up   11 mug   12 mud   13 not
14 nut   15 hut   16 hot   17 tug   18 cut   19 cup
20 cop

Exercise 2: Number from 1–7

Follow the usual procedure, or see the notes on page 10.

Answers

Transcript 🔊 **1.26** (0 mins, 48 secs)

1 mud   2 cog   3 hug   4 mug   5 nut   6 gum   7 hut

1 cut   2 cup   3 can   4 cot   5 cap   6 up   7 cat

Exercise 3: Listen and tick

Follow the usual procedure, or for faster classes, use the alternative below.

Faster classes: Instead of playing the CD, say a sentence containing one word from each pair, for example;
*I heard a loud **pop** from the gun.* (Students tick *pop*)
*There's a big **cat** sitting on my wall.* (Students tick *cat*)
*I think a **hog** is a kind of animal.* (Students tick *hog*), etc.
Students do not have to understand the sentences you say. What they do have to do is to pick out the word from the stream of speech. As an alternative or extra activity to ticking the word, students could simply raise their hands as the word is spoken, or repeat it at the end of the sentence.

Answers

Transcript 🔊 **1.27** (0 mins, 43 secs)

pup   cap   hog   gun   tug   nut   top up

hut   mug   op   cup   cut   hug   pop up

Exercise 4: Trace and write

Show students how to write lower-case *c* and *v*. Remind students about letters with decenders: *g* and *p*. Then follow the usual procedure.

Exercise 5: Read and label

Ask different students to read a word each. With students' pens down, teach/elicit the word for each picture. Then set the task. Monitor and give help where necessary. Make sure students are copying correctly and using good handwriting techniques. If students' handwriting is very weak, they will probably need more space to write the answers – give out lined paper or ask students to write in their notebooks. Elicit answers and write them on the board.

Answers

1 cup   **2** mug   **3** tin   **4** nut   **5** gum

Exercise 6: Find the words

Ask different students to read a word or phrase from the four at the top of the page. Set the task. Students complete individually, then compare answers with a partner. Monitor and give help where necessary. Elicit answers, preferably using an OHT/IWB.

> **Methodology note**
>
> This is a new activity so will need careful setting. Decide how you want students to complete it; they can either circle the target words in the visuals, or draw lines from the printed word to the word in the visual.

Exercise 7: Find the different word

Follow the usual procedure, but note that as there is an extra column in the table, you might need to allow extra time – 15 seconds instead of 10. For weaker classes, you may need even more time.

Answers

can	CAN	can	cat	can
TOP-UP	top-up	(top-up)	Top-up	Top-Up
mug	MUG	mug	(gum)	Mug
(hut)	nut	NUT	Nut	nut
Cup	CUP	Cup	cup	(cap)

Exercise 8: Separate the words

Exploit the visuals for the words *hug* and *cut*. Ask students to put their pens down. Read out the answers (words) in the first row. Students listen and look at the row of words. Then allow students to write the separate words. Repeat with each row.

Students complete individually, then compare answers with a partner. Monitor and give help where necessary. Encourage students to copy out the words correctly; it might be better to do this in a notebook or on a piece of paper so they have more space. For feedback, ask different students to read out a row of words each. Write the words on the board for students to check.

Answers

can / cap / cop / cut / cog / cup
mug / mad / men / map / mid
dog / dim / den / dam / dan
had / him / hat / hot / hug / hut

Exercise 9: Read key words

The suggested procedure is the same as for Unit 7, Exercise 7. This means students should now be familiar with it, so the activity will not take so long to set up. Set the task. With a partner, students take it in turns to read one word from the first line:

    S1: can
    S2: up
    S1: did
    S2: had

Play the CD for the first line. Ask students if they got any of the words wrong. Elicit the correct pronunciation of each word. Repeat the procedure for lines 2–4. Play the CD for all four lines with students following in their books. If you wish, you can do further practice of the words using flashcards.

> **Transcript** 🎧 **1.28** (1 min, 12 secs)
>
> | can | up | did | had | not | got | lot | him | let |
> |---|---|---|---|---|---|---|---|---|
> | GET | DID | HIM | CAN | ON | IN | UP | IT | GOT |
> | AN | IN | ON | UP | GOT | HIM | CAN | LOT | LET | DID |
> | at | am | in | it | up | get | can | got | get | did |
> | let | up | can |

Closure

Students' books should be closed. Use an OHT/IWB to show all the visuals from the lesson. See if students can remember the word or label for each visual.

9 B S

Objectives

By the end of the lesson, students should be able to:

- associate sight and sound of the letters *b* and *s* as capitals and lower case in a variety of typefaces;
- recognize words containing the two target letters in a variety of typefaces;
- demonstrate understanding of e-mail addresses;
- demonstrate understanding of previously learnt numbers 1–25;
- demonstrate recognition of previously learnt letters, words and names.

Adaptations

Faster/mixed-ability classes	Directed self-study
There are suggestions for faster classes in the notes below for the Introduction and for Exercise 9. As in previous units, you could start with Exercise 3 as a test, and go back to the earlier exercises only if necessary.	Go over the sounds for *b* and *s*. Tell student(s) which exercises to do. Remind them that they can replay the CD, or pause it, if they wish. Remind student(s) how to read e-mail addresses (Exercise 9).

Words for revision
(also available as flashcards)

Ann	Bill	Bob	Dan	Dot	Hal	Mac
Meg	Moll	Nat	Pam	Pat	Peg	Ted
Tim	Tom	up	Vic			

New letters/words for this lesson
(also available as flashcards)

B b /b/   S s /s/

bad	bag	bed	beg	big	bin	bit
bug	bun	bus	but	Cab	cub	Deb
hub	sad	Sal	Sam	sat nav	Seb	set
sip	sit	sum	sun	tub	us	

Introduction

Use flashcards to revise all the letters taught in Units 2–9: *a t i n*; *e p*; *m d*; *o*; *g v*; *h l*; *u c*. Elicit which letters are vowels, and which are consonants. Students now know the five basic vowel letters. Write them on the board. Teach the new letters *b* and *s*.

Faster classes: Ask students if they know any words in English beginning with each letter.

Exercise 1: Read and say

Follow the usual procedure. Revise the numbers 1–25 and teach the new numbers 26 and 27. As there are quite a lot of words to deal with in the last section, you can divide the words into sets of five. Deal with each set one at a time, before going on to the next set of five.

Exercise 2: Number from 1–7

Follow the usual procedure.

Answers

Exercise 3: Listen and tick

Follow the usual procedure. Some of these pairs of words are quite challenging, so be prepared to replay each pair two or three times, if necessary. Once you have given feedback on the correct answers, replay the whole exercise again on the CD, with students studying the pairs of words in their books.

Answers

Exercise 4: Trace and write

Follow the usual procedure. Demonstrate how to write the letter *b*, explaining that it is a tall letter with an ascender. Remind students about the descender on the letter *g* in the word *big*.

Exercise 5: Read and label

Ask students if they have a sat nav (satellite navigation system) in their cars. *Is it good? Do they like it?* Make sure students' pens are down. Teach/elicit the word for each picture. Then set the task. Students write the words individually, then compare answers with a partner. Monitor and give help where necessary.

Answers

1 sat nav   **2** bed   **3** bug   **4** SIM   **5** bag

Exercise 6: Find the different word

Follow the usual procedure.

Answers

sun	sum	sum	sum
but	**but**	bit	but
bad	bad	bed	bad
sad	sap	SAD	sad
bug	big	big	big

Exercise 7: Separate the words

Exploit the visual and teach the word *sunset*. Remind students to work from left to right, then follow the procedure from Unit 8, Exercise 8.

Answers

bin / bag / beg / bud / bug / bus / but
sit / sun / sad / set / sum / sip
gun / got / gum / get
bus / sun / but / tug / tap

Exercise 8: Read the names

Remind students that names in English begin with a capital letter. Ask students to look at the first line of names. Play the CD for the first line only. With a partner, students take it in turns to read and say each name. Monitor and give help where necessary. Repeat the procedure for the second line. Replay the CD for both the lines, with students following in their books. Practise any names students had difficulty in pronouncing. If you have time, you could spend a minute or so telling students which names are for men and which are for women. Some names could be male or female.

Exercise 9: Read and say the e-mail addresses, then listen and check

Remind students about the e-mail addresses they saw in Unit 5. Elicit how to say the e-mail addresses for Dan and Bill. Play the CD for the first two addresses only. Ask students to repeat the addresses. Now ask students to look at the address book extract. With a partner, students practise reading the addresses aloud. Then play the CD from the beginning.

Weaker classes: This can be done one address at a time.

Faster classes: Students try the first three addresses, then listen and check. Pause the CD, then students try the next three addresses. For further practice, you can set up the following pairwork activity:

S1: What's Dan's e-mail address?
S2: (It's) Dan at Mac dot com

Exercise 10: Read, then listen and check

Tell students to read down the columns (on a bus, in a bus). With a partner, students take it in turns to try to read a phrase aloud. Monitor, but do not confirm or correct at this stage. Play the CD. Ask different students to read out a phrase each. Practise pronunciation with the class. Finally, replay the CD with students following in their books.

Closure

Elicit the five vowel letters and sounds.

10 R

Objectives

By the end of the lesson, students should be able to:

- associate sight and sound of the letter *r* as capital and lower case in a variety of typefaces;
- recognize words containing the target letter in a variety of typefaces;
- demonstrate understanding of the adjectives *red* and *big*;
- demonstrate recognition of previously learnt letters, words and names.

Adaptations

Faster/mixed-ability classes	Directed self-study
There are suggestions for faster classes in the notes below for Exercise 9. As in previous units, you could start with Exercise 3 as a test, and go back to the earlier exercises only if necessary.	Go over the sound for *r*. Tell student(s) which exercises to do. Remind them that they can replay the CD, or pause it, if they wish.

Notes on new sounds

Make sure that the *r* sound is pronounced as a lateral, not overarticulated or trilled, rolled or uvular.

Words for revision
(also available as flashcards)

bad	bag	big	Bob	bug	hut	lab
led	lip	lot	Mac	man	pen	pet
sad	Sal	Seb	us	vat	vet	

New letters/words for this lesson
(also available as flashcards)

R r /r/

Arab	rag	ram	ran	rap	rat	red
rep	rid	rig	rim	rip	rob	rod
Ron	rub	rug	run	rut		

Introduction

Revise *p* and *b*. You can spend some time either now, or later on in the lesson (after Exercise 3), getting students to discriminate between the sounds of the letters *p* and *b*. Write the following words on the board/IWB (or use an OHT or flashcards):

p	*b*
1 pet	**2** bet
3 peg	**4** beg
5 pig	**6** big
7 pin	**8** bin
9 pen	**10** Ben
11 nip	**12** nib
13 hop	**14** hob
15 cap	**16** cab

Remind students how to pronounce the letters *p* and *b*. Choose between one or more of the following activities:
- **Students listen and repeat some of the words.**
- **Say one of the words at random; students say the number – this can also be done as pairwork.**
- **Say a number at random; students say the word – this can also be done as pairwork.**
- **Look at the pairs of words in order. Say one word from the pair. Students say which one it is. Again, this can be done as pairwork.**
- **With a partner, one student says the odd-numbered words in the first column, the other student says the even-numbered words.**

Exercise 1: Read and say

Introduce students to the sound of the letter *r*. Exploit the visual and teach the phrase *red bus*. Ask students to point out anything else in the classroom which is red: *a pen, a pencil, an item of clothing, a book,* etc. Follow the usual procedure for this exercise. However, when you get to section four, ask students to look for two names (*Rod* and *Ron*). This is an introduction to the reading sub-skill of scanning. Students might also say *Arab*. Explain that this is not really a name, but with words like *Arab*, *England* and *English*, we also need a capital letter.

Methodology note

In the third section, students are introduced to their first two-syllable word: *Arab*. On the CD, both *a*'s are pronounced the same way as /æ/, in order not to confuse the students. See the note in the Introduction (page 8) on unstressed syllables.

Exercise 2: Number from 1–7

Follow the usual procedure.

Answers

Exercise 3: Listen and tick

Follow the usual procedure.

Answers

Exercise 4: Trace and write

Follow the usual procedure.

Exercise 5: Read and label

Follow the usual procedure.

Answers

1 red   2 rag   3 rat   4 rug   5 run

Exercise 6: Read the names

Play the CD; pause after each name for students to repeat. Practise pronunciation with the class, chorally, then individually.

Exercise 7: Read, then listen and check

With a partner, students take it in turns to try to read a phrase aloud. Make sure students are reading down the columns. Monitor, but do not confirm or correct at this stage. Play the CD. Ask different students to read out a phrase each. Practise pronunciation with the class. Finally, replay the CD with students following in their books.

Methodology note

Students are introduced to the pattern *adjective + noun*. You should not try to explain this grammar point now, but just check students use the words in the correct order in phrases such as *red bus*, *big pen*, etc.

Exercise 8: Find the different word

Follow the usual procedure.

Answers

RAM	RAM	ROM	RAM
red	red	red	rod
run	ran	run	run
rid	rib	rib	rib

Exercise 9: Find words from Units 9 and 10

Use an OHT/IWB to set the task. Make sure students understand they can only find words from left to right, or top-down.

Faster classes: Once you have given feedback on the answers, ask students to rewrite the words as lower case.

Answers

Closure

Ask students to draw the following, either in their notebooks or on the board: a red pen, a big pen, a red rug, a big bug, a sad man, a red sun, a red bag.

Objectives

By the end of the lesson, students should be able to:

- associate sight and sound of the letters *y*, *w* and *j* as capitals and lower case in a variety of typefaces;
- recognize words containing the three target letters in a variety of typefaces;
- read aloud three-syllable place names and short phrases composed of the target letters and letters previously learnt;
- demonstrate recognition of previously learnt letters, words and names.

Adaptations

Faster/mixed-ability classes	Directed self-study
As in previous units, you could start with Exercise 3 as a test, and go back to the earlier exercises only if necessary.	Go over the sounds for *y*, *w* and *j*. Tell student(s) which exercises to do. Remind them that they can replay the CD, or pause it, if they wish.

Notes on new sounds

Make sure you pronounce the sounds of the letters with minimal voicing. *J* is a voiced affricate (contrasting with unvoiced *ch*), which may be difficult for some students. Other students may say hard *g* /g/ instead of the voiced affricate /ʤ/.

Words for revision
(also available as flashcards)

at	@	bed	dog	gig	hut	lot
map	not	on	pan	pen	red	rib
run	set	sun	sunset	Tim	tub	vat

New letters/words for this lesson
(also available as flashcards)

Y y /J/   W w /w/   J j /ʤ/

Arabic	Basra	jab	jam	Jan	Japan
Jen	jet	jig	Jim	job	jug
Lebanon	Madrid	web	wet	win	wit
yam	yen	yes	yet	yob	

Introduction

The words for revision cover the first ten units. Write words from the list on the board/IWB (or use flashcards or an OHT). Choose between these activities:

- students listen and repeat selected words;
- designated students read out words;
- show students an example word, but do not read it out; students find words beginning with the same letter. Monitor and evaluate students' responses, correcting as necessary.

Exercise 1: Read and say

Introduce students to the sounds of the letters *y*, *w*, and *j*. Exploit the visual of the jet. Follow the usual procedure for this exercise. To provide more practice in scanning – and to reinforce the fact that names begin with a capital letter – when you get to the third section, ask students to spot the name (*Japan*). Do the same for the fourth section – where there are five (*Sam, Japan, Jim, Jan, Jen*). Point out that there is a dot on the lower-case *j*, but not on the capital.

Transcript ⚫ 1.40 (2 mins, 54 secs)

1 y	2 w	3 j	4 Y	5 W	6 J			
1 y	2 w	3 s	4 w	5 v	6 y	7 j	8 g	9 b
10 p	11 n	12 m	13 w	14 Y	15 V	16 W		
17 G	18 J	19 Y	20 W	21 J				

1 yen	2 yes	3 yet	4 yob	5 web	6 wed	7 wet
8 win	9 wit	10 jab	11 jam	12 jet	13 jig	
14 job	15 jug	16 Japan				

1 yet	2 jet	3 yob	4 job	5 yes	6 rug	7 jug
8 jig	9 win	10 web	11 wet	12 vet	13 yen	
14 van	15 jab	16 lab	17 Sam	18 jam	19 Japan	
20 Jim	21 Jan	22 Jen				

Exercise 2: Number from 1–7

Follow the usual procedure.

Answers

Transcript 🔊 1.41 (0 mins, 54 secs)

1 job	2 yen	3 yam	4 jet	5 jam	6 yet	7 yes
1 wet	2 jug	3 win	4 job	5 web	6 jig	7 wit

Exercise 3: Listen and tick

Ask students to find the two names (*Jen* and *Jan*). Follow the usual procedure. Replay any difficult pairs, such as *Jan* and *Jen*, if students have difficulty.

Answers

Transcript 🔊 1.42 (0 mins, 28 secs)

yet	job	yet	jet	wet
jug	yam	yes	web	Jan

Exercise 4: Trace and write

First, note the descenders on *y* and *j* and the dot on lower-case *j*. Remind students that *t* is taller, having an ascender. Then follow the usual procedure.

Exercise 5: Read and label

Follow the usual procedure.

Answers

1 wet **2** yen **3** jug **4** jam

Exercise 6: Find the different word

Follow the usual procedure.

Answers

yes	(yet)	yes	YES
job	job	job	(yob)
win	win	(vim)	win
(jab)	lab	lab	lab

Exercise 7: Read the names

Remind the students that names begin with a capital letter. Point out the way capital *J* is handwritten with a top stroke, in contrast to the printed version. Play the CD. With a partner, students take it in turns to read and say each name. Replay the CD. Practise any names students had difficulty in pronouncing. If there is time, point out which names are for men and which for women.

Transcript 🔊 1.43 (0 mins, 28 secs)

Jim	Jan	Hal	Dot	Al	Meg	Len	Ben	Val
Jen	Win							

Exercise 8: Read, then listen and check

Play the CD for the first section. Students follow each word in their books from left to right. Students take it in turns to read each word. Monitor, but do not confirm or correct. Ask different students to read out a word each. Practise pronunciation with the whole class. Repeat this procedure for the second and third section. For the third section, make sure students are reading down the columns. As a final phase, replay the CD with students following in their books.

Methodology note

There are words and phrases here that students will not understand if they are at a low language level. Focus on saying the words and do not try to explain what each phrase means.

Transcript 🔊 1.44 (1 min, 29 secs)

Jap-an	Mad-rid	Bas-ra	Leb-an-on	Can-a-da	
Arab-ic					
Japan	Madrid	Basra	Lebanon	Canada	Arabic
yes, yes, yes	a JAL jet		win yen		tin can
but not yet	not us		yen in Japan		web jam
747 jet	a job in Japan		wed him		get a lot

Exercise 9: Separate the words

Follow the usual procedure.

Answers

jet / jam / job / jig / jab / jug
web / wit / wet / wed / win
yob / yes / yet / yen / yes
ran / rid / red / rim / rub / rug

Closure

Students' books should be closed. Use an OHT/IWB to show all the visuals from the lesson. See if students can remember the label for each visual.

Objectives
By the end of the lesson, students should be able to:

- associate sight and sound of the letters *f*, *x* and *z* as capitals and lower case in a variety of typefaces;

- recognize words containing the three target letters in a variety of typefaces;

- read aloud two- and three-syllable names of companies composed of the target letters and letters previously learnt;

- demonstrate recognition of previously learnt letters, words and names.

Adaptations

Faster/mixed-ability classes	Directed self-study
As in previous units, you could start with Exercise 3 as a test, and go back to the earlier exercises only if necessary.	Go over the sounds for *f*, *x* and *z*. Tell student(s) which exercises to do. Remind them that they can replay the CD, or pause it, if they wish.

Words for revision
(also available as flashcards)

Arab	bad	bus	cat	dog	hot	jet
lid	nit	on	pen	run	sun	up
van	web	wet	yet			

New letters/words for this lesson
(also available as flashcards)

F f /f/   X x /ks/   Z z /z/

box	disk	exam	exit	Exxon	fan	fat
fax	fed	Fedex	fig	fit	fix	fizz
fog	fox	fun	if	jazz	Lexus	mix
ox	Oz	sax	sex	six	tax	Texaco
Texas	wax	zed	zigzag			

Introduction

The words for revision above cover the first ten units. Write words from the list on the board/IWB (or use flashcards or an OHT). Choose between these activities:

- **students listen and repeat selected words;**
- **individual students read out words;**
- **show students an example word, but do not read it out; students find words beginning with the same letter. Monitor and evaluate students' responses, correcting as necessary.**

Exercise 1: Read and say

Introduce students to the sounds of the letters *f*, *x* and *z*. Exploit the visual of the box, monitoring for the correct pronunciation of *b* and *x* (/b/ and /ks/). Follow the usual procedure for this exercise.

Methodology note

Make sure you pronounce the sounds of the letters with minimum voicing. *X* is a consonant cluster (/k/+/s/) which may be difficult for some students. Make sure they do not put an intrusive vowel between /k/ and /s/. In the third and fourth sections, make sure that students produce short vowels, especially /ɪ/, not /iː/.

Transcript 1.45 (3 mins, 46 secs)

1 f	2 x	3 z	4 F	5 X	6 Z				

1 f	2 x	3 z	4 s	5 v	6 f	7 x	8 s	9 g	10 j
11 f	12 w	13 y	14 S	15 X	16 W	17 F	18 J		
19 Z	20 G	21 V							

1 fan	2 fat	3 fed	4 fig	5 fit	6 fix	7 fizz
8 jazz	9 fox	10 fog	11 fun	12 if	13 box	
14 sex	15 six	16 wax	17 tax	18 mix	19 fax	
20 zigzag	21 exam	22 exit	23 ox	24 Oz		

1 fox	2 mix	3 tax	4 sax	5 six	6 sex	7 fax
8 fit	9 exam	10 fat	11 fun	12 if	13 wax	
14 fan	15 zed	16 exit	17 zigzag	18 fig	19 jazz	
20 box	21 fizz	22 fix				

Exercise 2: Number from 1–7

Follow the usual procedure.

Answers

1 six	**2** exit	**3** fizz	**4** exam	**5** box	**6** fix	**7** jazz
1 fan	**2** fit	**3** if	**4** fat	**5** fun	**6** fog	**7** zigzag

Exercise 3: Listen and tick

Ask students to find the name in the items (*Oz*). Do not tell them to look for a word beginning with a capital letter unless they need help. By now, they should not need telling. Point out that *Oz* only has one *z* because it is a name, not a word. Follow the usual procedure. Replay any difficult pairs if students have difficulty hearing distinctions.

Answers

tax	fox	fan	six	fizz
fig	jazz	Oz	sax	fin

Exercise 4: Trace and write

First, point out the ascender on *f*, and demonstrate on the board that *z* is handwritten with three straight lines and two acute angles – not a curve at the top like the number *2*. Then follow the usual procedure. Make sure all letters have been written on the line, except *p*, *g* and *j*, and that *f* has been written on the line with an ascender.

Exercise 5: Read and label

Follow the usual procedure.

Answers

1 zigzag **2** fan **3** sax **4** six **5** fox

Exercise 6: Read the computer words

Play the CD. Students follow in their books. Go round the class, asking different students to read each word aloud. Remind them that @ = *at*, if necessary. Then, using an OHT/IWB, point to a word and invite a response, first from volunteers, and then from chosen students. Ask the students to work with a partner to test each other by taking turns to point to an item and asking their partner to read it aloud. Then reverse the process: taking turns, one student reads a word and the partner has to point to it.

> **Methodology note**
>
> As the @ symbol comes first, return to this later if students have difficulty remembering it. They may recall it as they work on the other items.

@	web	RAM	rom	dot com	net	fax	box

Exercise 7: Read, then listen and check

Students look at the pictures. Play the CD and ask students to follow each word in their books from left to right. Students take it in turns to read each word. Monitor, but do not confirm or correct. Practise pronunciation with the whole class. As a final phase, replay the CD with students following in their books.

ex-it	exit	Fed-Ex	FedEx	EXX-ON	EXXON
zig-zag	zigzag	Tex-a-co	Texaco	LEX-US	LEXUS

Exercise 8: Find and circle words with *f* and *x*, then listen and check

Students work individually or with a partner to circle the words. Ask them how many they have found. Do not correct if there are any wrong totals, but play the CD, with pauses if necessary, to allow students to locate each word. They are recorded in the right order – left to right, top to bottom.

Answers

Sam Cox   Exco Inc   PO Box 659   Dallas   Texas
TX 345812   Tel: 214 5091 487   Fax: 214 5091 763
e-mail: sam dot cox at exco dot net
web: www dot exco dot com

Closure

Students' books should be closed. Use an OHT/IWB to show all the visuals from the lesson. See if students can remember the label for each visual.

13 K C K

Objectives
By the end of the lesson, students should be able to:

- associate sight and sound of the letter *k* and the letter combination *ck* as capitals and lower case in a variety of typefaces;

- recognize words containing the target letters in a variety of typefaces;

- read aloud one- and two-syllable words composed of the target letters and letters previously learnt;

- demonstrate recognition of previously learnt letters, words and names;

- demonstrate awareness that single *k* begins a word, and *ck* comes at the end of a word or syllable.

Adaptations

Faster/mixed-ability classes	Directed self-study
As this is the first unit with words of four letters or more, check whether students can do sections three and four of Exercise 1.	Carefully go over the sound for *k* and *ck*. Tell student(s) which exercises to do. Remind them that they can replay the CD, or pause it, if they wish.

Words for revision
(also available as flashcards)

fax	fit	fizz	jazz	mix	six	tax
wax	zed	zigzag				

New letters/words for this lesson
(also available as flashcards)

K k /k/   ck /k/

back	backpack	deck	dock	duck	keg
kick	kid	kin	kit	lack	lick
lock	luck	muck	pack	pick	rack
rock	sack	sick	tick	wick	

Introduction
Write words from the revision list on the board/IWB (or use flashcards or an OHT). **Choose between these activities:**
- **students listen and repeat selected words;**
- **designated students read out words;**
- **show students an example word, but do not read it out; students find words beginning with the same letter. Monitor and evaluate students' responses, correcting as necessary.**

Exercise 1: Read and say

Introduce students to the sound of the letter *k* and the written combination *ck*. As usual, ensure you make sure you pronounce the sounds of the letters with minimum voicing. Exploit the visual (*sock*). Follow the usual procedure for this exercise. Check pronunciation, making sure that the /k/ sound is pronounced as a velar plosive, not as a glottal.

Transcript ⏺ 2.1 (3 mins, 16 secs)

1 k   2 K   3 c   4 ck

1 k   2 ck   3 c   4 s   5 z   6 x   7 g   8 j   9 v
10 w   11 b   12 p   13 y   14 j   15 C   16 K   17 X
18 R   19 T   20 K   21 S

1 keg   2 kid   3 kin   4 kit   5 kick   6 back   7 deck
8 dock   9 duck   10 lick   11 lock   12 luck   13 pack
14 pick   15 rock   16 sack   17 sick   18 sock
19 tick   20 wick

1 rock   2 pick   3 back   4 pack   5 sack   6 kid
7 kit   8 duck   9 dock   10 deck   11 luck   12 lack
13 lick   14 sick   15 tick   16 sock   17 kin   18 keg
19 wick   20 kick   21 lock   22 muck   23 rack
24 backpack

Exercise 2: Number from 1–7
Follow the usual procedure.

Answers

Exercise 3: Listen and tick

Follow the usual procedure. Replay any difficult pairs if students have difficulty hearing distinctions.

Answers

Exercise 4: Trace and write

Note the ascender on *k*. Then follow the usual procedure. Make sure all letters have been written on the line and *k* has its ascender. Point out that *k* begins a word and *ck* comes at the end of a word or syllable, e.g., *backpack*. A word cannot start with *ck*, and it cannot end with *k* alone.

Exercise 5: Read and label

Follow the usual procedure.

Answers

1 sack   **2** duck   **3** rock   **4** backpack   **5** lock

Exercise 6: Read the key words at speed

Draw attention to the visual of the clock and tell students that *tick tock* is the English for the sound of a clock. As this is a speed test revising words already encountered, the objective is for each student to read the words accurately, as fast as possible. Ensure students read *at* twice; this will reinforce the sound-symbol connection.

Go through these stages:
- Using an OHT/IWB, the class says each word after the teacher. Or use the CD. Aim for pace here. If not using the CD, remember to pronounce the first word, *a*, as /æ/, not as a schwa (/ə/). Use citation pronunciation throughout.
- Pairwork: One student times his/her partner and then the roles reverse. Students note their partner's time. Demonstrate this with a student first.
- Students report back on the time taken by their partner.

Exercise 7: Read the names

Ask students to look at the names for a moment, to work out how to say them. Play the CD and ask students to follow the pronunciation. Ask for a volunteer to read each name aloud. Monitor. If correct, ask selected students to repeat what the volunteer said. Get students to listen to each other in this activity. If incorrect, ask for another volunteer. Monitor, and if correct, ask selected students to repeat what the volunteer said. If no one can do it, then you can provide the model, pointing to a student to repeat after you.

Exercise 8: Read, then listen and check

Draw attention to the visual of the padlock. Play the CD and ask students to follow each word in their books, reading down the columns. Students take it in turns to read each phrase. Monitor, but do not correct. Practise pronunciation with the whole class. As a final phase, replay the CD with students following in their books.

Exercise 9: Separate the words

Follow the usual procedure. Allow time in the lesson planning for slow writers. Give out sheets of paper for poor writers, as they tend to have large writing.

Answers

kick / lock / pack / back / luck
kid / kin / kit / kick / kid / kick
fizz / zed / jazz / zen
six / fax / box / sex / fix / tax / wax

Exercise 10: Find words from Units 12 and 13

Use this exercise as the Closure. Follow the usual procedure. Explain that the students only need to look for words in the wordsearch – not in the visuals accompanying it.

Answers

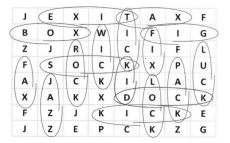

Closure

Use Exercise 10 – the wordsearch – as the Closure.

Q U T H W H

Objectives

By the end of the lesson, students should be able to:

- associate sight and sound of the letter combinations *qu*, *th* and *wh* as capitals and lower case in a variety of typefaces;
- recognize words containing the letter combinations in a variety of typefaces;
- read aloud one-syllable words composed of the target letter combinations and letters previously learnt;
- demonstrate recognition of previously learnt letters, words and names.

Adaptations

Faster/mixed-ability classes	Directed self-study
There are some five letter words which need careful checking. Start with Exercise 3 as a test, and go back to the earlier exercises if necessary.	There are some five letter words which need careful checking before proceeding. Go over the sounds for *qu*, *th* and *wh*. Tell student(s) which exercises to do. Remind them that they can replay the CD, or pause it, if they wish.

Words for revision

(also available as flashcards)

back	backpack	deck	dock	duck	keg
kick	kid	kin	kit	lack	lick
lock	luck	muck	neck	pack	pick
rack	rock	sack	sick	tick	

New letters/words for this lesson

(also available as flashcards)

qu /kw/   th /ð/   wh /w/

quick	quid	quip	quit	than	that	them
then	this	when	whim	whip	whiz	with

Introduction

Write words from the revision list on the board/IWB (or use flashcards or an OHT). Choose between these activities:

- **students listen and repeat selected words;**
- **designated students read out words;**
- **using the OHT/IWB, students find words which begin with the same letter as an example which the teacher points out (without reading aloud), and read them aloud. Monitor and evaluate students' responses, correcting as necessary.**

Exercise 1: Read and say

Introduce students to the sound of the letters. As usual, ensure you make sure you pronounce the sounds of the letters with minimum voicing. Exploit the visual (*quit*). Follow the usual procedure for this exercise.

Methodology note

All the words containing *th* in this unit have voiced *th*. Teach voiced *th* /ð/ only, and exclude the voiceless version /θ/ (e.g., *th* in *thatch*). Check and make sure that the *th* sound is pronounced as a voiced dental fricative, not as an alveolar *s* or *z*.

Teach *wh* as the same as *w*, i.e., /w/, not /hw/ as this is obsolete in RP. As usual, when providing models, avoid extending the sound to include a schwa-like vowel.

Teach *qu* as /k/ and /w/, then join the two sounds.

Transcript ⏺ 2.7 (2 mins, 37 secs)

1 qu	**2** th	**3** wh	**4** Qu	**5** Th	**b** Wh			

1 qu	**2** k	**3** c	**4** ck	**5** qu	**6** t	**7** th	**8** wh	**9** w
10 qu	**11** th	**12** Qu	**13** Th	**14** Wh	**15** C	**16** Qu		
17 Th								

1 quid	**2** quip	**3** quit	**4** quick	**5** than	**6** that
7 them	**8** then	**9** this	**10** when	**11** whim	
12 whip	**13** whiz	**14** with			

1 quip	**2** whip	**3** this	**4** with	**5** them	**6** then
7 quid	**8** quick	**9** that	**10** hat	**11** this	**12** win
13 whim	**14** whiz	**15** with	**16** wit		
17 wick					

Exercise 2: Number from 1–7

Follow the usual procedure.

Answers

> **1** then **2** quick **3** when **4** with **5** quit **6** this
> **7** whip

Exercise 3: Listen and tick

Follow the usual procedure. Replay any difficult pairs if students have difficulty hearing distinctions.

Answers

> quick   then   them   with   then   win
> quip   with   quick   kid   quit   this

Exercise 4: Trace and write

First remind students of the ascender on *h* and of the fact that *t* is a tall letter but not as tall as *h*. Then follow the usual procedure. Point out that *q* always goes with *u* in English words.

Exercise 5: Find the different word

Follow the usual procedure.

Answers

when	WHEN	when	(then)
that	(than)	that	that
quick	quick	quick	(quit)
(then)	them	them	them

Exercise 6: Read, then listen and check

Draw attention to the visual. Then follow the usual procedure.

> Quit   Quick   When   Quick   Quick   When   quip
> that   them   when   quick   this   get   got   with
> than   but   bit   can   did   quick   quit   then
> when   quip   quit   Quick   this   whip

Exercise 7: Separate the words

Follow the usual procedure. Allow time in the lesson planning for slow writers. Give out sheets of paper for poor writers, as they tend to have large writing.

Answers

when / then / them / than / win / with whim / wit / with / when quit / when / quid / them / than / then

Exercise 8: Find words from Unit 14

Use this exercise as the Closure. Follow the usual procedure.

Answers

Q	U	I	T	S	G	U	Z
U	F	T	H	E	N	W	H
I	Q	U	I	P	W	H	K
C	U	C	S	W	H	I	P
K	I	B	W	H	E	Z	K
J	D	T	H	A	N	E	J
F	X	W	I	T	H	A	T
T	H	E	M	D	V	A	L

Closure

Use Exercise 8 – the wordsearch – as the Closure.

15 | S H | C H | T C H

Objectives

By the end of the lesson, students should be able to:

- associate sight and sound of the letter combinations *sh*, *ch* and *tch* in lower case and with an initial capital in a variety of typefaces;

- recognize words containing the letter combinations in a variety of typefaces;

- read aloud one-syllable words composed of the target letter combinations and letters previously learnt, and simple phrases containing words with the new letter combinations;

- demonstrate recognition of previously learnt letters, words and names.

Adaptations

Faster/mixed-ability classes	Directed self-study
As in previous units, you could start with Exercise 3 as a test, and go back to the earlier exercises only if necessary.	Go over the sounds for *sh*, *ch* and *tch*. Tell student(s) they don't have to do every activity, as there are many. Remind them that they can replay the CD, or pause it, if they wish.

Words for revision
(also available as flashcards)

quick	quid	quip	quit	than	that	them
then	this	when	whim	whip	whiz	with

New letters/words for this lesson
(also available as flashcards)

sh /ʃ/ ch /tʃ/ tch /tʃ/

cash	catch	chap	chat	chin	chip	chock
chop	dash	dish	ditch	fetch	fish	hatch
hush	itch	lash	latch	mash	match	much
mush	patch	pitch	posh	sash	shed	shin
ship	shock	shop	shot	shut	such	which
wish						

Introduction

Write words from the revision list on the board/IWB (or use flashcards or an OHT). Choose between these activities:

- students listen and repeat selected words
- designated students read out words
- show students an example word, but do not read it out; students find words beginning with the same letter. Monitor and evaluate students' responses, correcting as necessary.

As this unit is quite long, you can either not do every exercise, or, reorder the exercises, e.g., do Exercise 5 in between the third and fourth sections of Exercise 1.

Exercise 1: Read and say

Introduce students to the sounds of the letter combinations. Use the method suggested in the Methodology note below, if necessary. As usual, ensure you pronounce the sounds of the letters with minimal voicing. Exploit the visual (*fish and chips*). Follow the usual procedure for this exercise. Point out that you write *ch* when the sound begins a word, and *tch* when it ends a word or syllable.

Methodology note

Check that the pronunciation of *sh* is distinguished from that of *ch*. If there are problems making the *sh – ch/tch* contrast, as there will be with speakers of certain languages, you can teach *ch* (which is usually the problem) by first getting students to say *t*, then *sh*. Then get them to join the two sounds.

1 sh **2** ch **3** tch **4** Sh **5** Ch

1 sh **2** ch **3** c **4** ck **5** s **6** sh **7** qu **8** wh
9 j **10** tch **11** y **12** Th **13** Ch **14** Sh **15** C
16 S **17** J

1 shed **2** ship **3** shop **4** shot **5** shock **6** shut
7 chap **8** chat **9** chin **10** chip **11** chop **12** cash
13 dash **14** dish **15** fish **16** posh **17** wish
18 much **19** such **20** which **21** itch **22** catch
23 match **24** patch

1 ship **2** chip **3** shop **4** chop **5** wish **6** which
7 cash **8** catch **9** posh **10** patch **11** dash
12 match **13** dish **14** shed **15** much **16** such
17 shut **18** chat **19** chin **20** shock **21** itch
22 pitch **23** ditch **24** fetch

Exercise 2: Number from 1–7

Follow the usual procedure.

Answers

1 shop **2** shut **3** dash **4** ship **5** cash **6** wish
7 shed

1 fetch **2** which **3** chop **4** chat **5** catch **6** chin
7 much

Exercise 3: Listen and tick

Follow the usual procedure. Replay (or say again) any difficult pairs, such as *mash* and *match*, if students have difficulty.

Answers

ship chin chop shock wish much hush

match lash catch dish which hatch itch

Exercise 4: Trace and write

As they have written them before, ask students what is special about writing the letter *h* (it has an ascender) and the letter *p* (it has a descender). Then follow the usual procedure.

Exercise 5: Read and label

Follow the usual procedure.

Answers

1 match **2** chips **3** ship **4** shop **5** dish

Exercise 6: Read, then listen and check

Draw attention to the visuals, but do not worry too much about meaning here. Then follow the usual procedure.

and AND & *and* & and And & and &

and	&
fish	which
chips	shop
shop	Which shop?
fish shop	Which man?
chip shop	Which box?
fish & chips	Which ship?
fish and chip shop	And which dish?
Which fish shop?	Which fish and chip shop?

Exercise 7: Find the different word

Follow the usual procedure.

Answers

and	&	ant	and
much	mush	much	much
which	which	WHICH	hitch
shop	ship	ship	ship
cash	catch	cash	cash

Exercise 8: Find words from Unit 15

Use this exercise as the closure phase. Follow the usual procedure.

Answers

W	M	X	A	N	D	R	C
H	U	S	H	E	D	J	A
I	C	H	S	H	I	P	T
C	H	O	P	J	S	C	C
H	G	P	O	S	H	H	H
C	A	S	H	X	Z	I	W
Z	M	A	T	C	H	P	Y
S	H	O	C	K	Q	U	K

Closure

Use Exercise 8 for this phase.

16

Objectives

By the end of the lesson, students should be able to:

- associate sight and sound of the letter combination *oo* in lower case and with an initial capital;

- contrast the sound *oo* as in *loot* with *o* as in *lot*;

- distinguish the sound of *o* in *lot* from *o* in *do* (see Exercise 6);

- recognize words containing *oo* and *o*;

- read aloud one-syllable words composed of the target letters and letters previously learnt, and simple phrases containing words using the new letter combination;

- demonstrate recognition of previously learnt letters, words and names.

Adaptations

Faster/mixed-ability classes	Directed self-study
As in previous units, you could start with Exercise 3 as a test, and go back to the earlier exercises only if necessary.	Go over the sounds for *oo* and *o*. Tell student(s) which exercises to do. Remind them that they can replay the CD, or pause it, if they wish.

Words for revision
(also available as flashcards)

cash	catch	chap	chat	chin	chip	chock
chop	dash	dish	ditch	fetch	fish	hatch
hush	itch	lash	latch	mash	match	much
mush	patch	pitch	posh	sash	shed	shin
ship	shock	shop	shot	shut	such	which
wish						

New letters/words for this lesson
(also available as flashcards)

oo /uː/

boo	boo hoo	boom	boot	do	food
fox	hoot	hot	loo	loot	lot
moo	moon	noon	not	Oo	posh
rom	roof	room	root	rot	shoot
shop	shot	sock	soon	too	toot
top	whoosh	zoo	zoom		

Introduction

Write words from the revision list on the board/IWB (or use flashcards or an OHT). Choose between these activities:

- students listen and repeat selected words;
- designated students read out words;
- show students an example word, but do not read it out; students find words beginning with the same letter.

Monitor and evaluate students' responses, correcting as necessary.

In this unit, only *oo* /uː/ is taught; *oo* /ʊ/ (e.g., *good*) is covered in Unit 47.

Exercise 1: Read and say

Introduce students to the sound of the letter *o* and the letter combination *oo*. The sound *oo* is the first long vowel the students have been introduced to. Make sure they differentiate between *o* and *oo*. Exploit the visual (*moon*). Follow the usual procedure for this exercise.

> **Transcript** 🔊 **2.15** (1 min, 36 secs)
>
> **1** o   **2** oo   **3** O   **4** Oo
>
> **1** o   **2** oo   **3** a   **4** e   **5** i   **6** u   **7** qu   **8** oo   **9** e   **10** o
>
> **1** lot   **2** loot   **3** shot   **4** shoot   **5** rot   **6** root   **7** zoo   **8** zoom
>
> **1** boo   **2** boot   **3** food   **4** loo   **5** moon   **6** noon   **7** roof   **8** room   **9** root   **10** shoot   **11** soon   **12** too   **13** zoo   **14** zoom

Exercise 2: Number from 1–7

Follow the usual procedure.

Answers

Exercise 3: Listen and tick

Follow the usual procedure. Replay (or say again) any difficult pairs if students have difficulty.

Answers

Exercise 4: Trace and write

Follow the usual procedure.

Exercise 5: Read and label

Follow the usual procedure.

Answers

1 boot   **2** roof   **3** zoom   **4** noon   **5** food

Exercise 6: Read, then listen and check

Set the first section (words numbered 1–7) as pairwork. Students read the words to each other in turn. Resolve any disagreements about pronunciation. Then follow the usual procedure. For the second section, make sure students read down the columns.

Exercise 7: Read the key words at speed

This is a revision of new and previously learnt words. Ask for volunteers to read out the words. Correct if necessary and get the class to repeat. If a student gets the pronunciation right, use him/her as a model. Get students to listen to him/her and to each other, rather than always being the model they listen to. For reinforcement, play the CD.

Exercise 8: Find the words

This is a simple correlation exercise to see if the students can recognize the target words in a new (cartoon) style. Ask students to read silently. Then, using an OHT/IWB to display the pictures, ask individual students to read the words in each speech bubble, paying critical attention to their responses.

Closure

Check what students have learnt by showing flashcards of the new words. Ask for volunteers or select students to respond. Reinforce with class repetition as appropriate, e.g., where an item appears to be difficult.

17 [E] [E] [E] [A]

Objectives

By the end of the lesson, students should be able to:

- associate sight and sound of the letter combinations *ee* and *ea* in lower case and with an initial capital;
- read aloud one-syllable words composed of the target letters and letters previously learnt;
- demonstrate recognition of previously learnt letters, words and names;
- recognize and read the numbers 20, 25, 30, 40, etc.;
- recognize and read *p* as in *30p* (*pence*).

Adaptations

Faster/mixed-ability classes	Directed self-study
As students are learning a second long vowel sound with two spellings, test ability using section four of Exercise 1 rather than the usual Exercise 3, unless it is a very good class.	Go over the two letter combinations *ee* and *ea* for the one sound /iː/. Tell student(s) which exercises to do. Remind them that they can replay the CD, or pause it, if they wish.

Words for revision
(also available as flashcards)

boo	boo hoo	boom	boot	do	food
fox	hoot	hot	loo	loot	lot
moo	moon	noon	not	Oo	posh
rom	roof	room	root	rot	shoot
shop	shot	sock	soon	too	toot
top	whoosh	zoo	zoom		

New letters/words for this lesson
(also available as flashcards)

ee /iː/   ea /iː/

beach	beak	bean	bee	beef	been	cheap
cheek	coffee	each	eat	eel	fee	feed
feet	keen	keep	meat	meet	neat	queen
read	sea	seat	see	seem	seen	sheep
tea	teach	team	teen	ten	week	wheat
wheel						

Introduction

Write words from the revision list on the board/IWB (or use flashcards or an OHT). Choose between these activities:

- **students listen and repeat selected words**
- **designated students read out words**
- **show students an example word, but do not read it out; students find words beginning with the same letter. Monitor and evaluate students' responses, correcting as necessary.**

Exercise 1: Read and say

Introduce the combinations *ee* and *ea* as representing the same sound /iː/. Exploit the visual for this. Get students to read what they can from the visual (they will be able to read most of the words). They will probably be able to infer *coffee* and *tea*. Show them how *ee* and *ea* represent the same sound. Then follow the usual procedure for this exercise.

Transcript ⏺ 2.20 (2 mins, 9 secs)

1 e   2 ee   3 e   4 ea

1 e   2 oo   3 ee   4 o   5 ea   6 e   7 u   8 i   9 Ee
10 Ea

1 ben   2 been   3 bean   4 ten   5 teen   6 team

1 bee   2 beef   3 been   4 feet   5 keep   6 meet
7 see   8 seem   9 seen   10 sheep   11 week
12 coffee   13 cheek   14 queen   15 tea   16 sea
17 eat   18 each   19 beach   20 read   21 cheap
22 meat   23 seat   24 wheat   25 teach

Exercise 2: Number from 1–7

Follow the usual procedure.

Answers

Transcript ⏺ 2.21 (0 mins, 25 secs)

1 queen   2 bee   3 beat   4 been   5 feet   6 fee
7 wheat

Exercise 3: Listen and tick

Follow the usual procedure. Replay (or say again) any difficult pairs if students have difficulty.

Answers

feed	cheek	read	meat	wheat	set	neat
keen	queen	each	beak	teach	eel	sheep

Exercise 4: Trace and write

Remind students that *d* and *b* are tall letters. Follow the usual procedure.

Exercise 5: Read and label

Follow the usual procedure.

Answers

1 meat **2** tea **3** seat **4** feet **5** sheep

Exercise 6: Read, then listen and check

As it's some time since students have done an activity on numbers, do some revision. Also distinguish between the letter *O* and the number *0*. Then follow the usual procedure.

pee	5p	10p	15p	20p	25p		
20	30	40	50	60	70	80	90
20p	30p	40p	50p	60p	70p	80p	90p

Exercise 7: Read the menu aloud, then listen and check

To enhance their comprehension and learning, students can learn the meanings of this food-related vocabulary. As there could be a problem with *beef* being the word for the meat from cows or bulls, and for the other food words, bring in visuals of food to reinforce meanings of all the words. Ask individual students to read word by word. With a partner, students read the menu to each other, helping each other. Monitor and correct. Play the CD, with students following in their books.

Eat at Poole Beach Coffee Shop

This week

Cup of hot tea	1.40
Mug of coffee	1.70

Salads	
beef	4.50
egg	3.80
cheese	3.90
fish	5.30
egg with cheese	6.20

+ VAT 15%

Exercise 8: Read the names

This exercise consolidates the target letter combinations and revises the letter combinations from other units. Play the CD. Students follow in their books. Get students to read back each name. Be prepared for problems with Quentin Hancock.

Dick Bean
Dee Boon
Viv Booth
Mick Cash
Ben Chan
Jim Choo
Liz Cox
Adam Dean
Sam Doon
Ann Fox
Quentin Hancock
Hal Keen
Dan Lee
Bob Moon
Jack Nash
Nick Read
Jan Seed

Closure

Use flashcards to review the new words from the unit.

18 B E M E

Objectives

By the end of the lesson students should be able to:

- read single *e* as /iː/ in subject pronouns, *the*, and the verb *be*;
- read single *e* as /e/ when followed by a consonant;
- read *ee* and *ea* as /iː/ in other cases (see Unit 17);
- read aloud one-syllable words that demonstrate these pronunciations of *e*;
- demonstrate recognition of previously learnt letters, words and names;
- recognize the symbol # as meaning *number*.

Adaptations

Faster/mixed-ability classes	Directed self-study
As in previous units, you could start with Exercise 3 as a test, and go back to the earlier exercises only if necessary.	Go over the sounds for *be* and *me*. Tell student(s) which exercises to do. Remind them that they can replay the CD, or pause it, if they wish.

Words for revision
(also available as flashcards)

beach	beak	bean	bee	beef	been	cheap
cheek	coffee	each	eat	eel	fee	feed
feet	keen	keep	meat	meet	neat	queen
read	sea	seat	see	seem	seen	sheep
tea	teach	team	teen	ten	week	wheat
wheel						

New letters/words for this lesson
(also available as flashcards)

be	bee	he	heap	hem	hen	me
sea	she	shed	sheet	we	weep	

Introduction

This unit covers the use of a single final *e* to represent /iː/ in pronouns (e.g., *me*, *she*), *the*, and *be*, and *ee* or *ea* to represent /iː/ in other cases (see Unit 17). It revises single *e* followed by a final consonant (/e/).

Write words from the revision list on the board/IWB (or use flashcards or an OHT). Choose between these activities:
- students listen and repeat selected words
- designated students read out words
- show students an example word, but do not read it out; students find words beginning with the same letter. Monitor and evaluate students' responses, correcting as necessary.

Exercise 1: Read and say

Introduce single *e* as representing the sound /iː/ in words like words *be* and *me*. These are exceptions to the way /iː/ is normally written. Remind students how /iː/ is written *ee* and *ea* in other contexts. Then follow the usual procedure for this exercise.

> **Transcript** 🔊 **2.26** (2 mins, 29 secs)
>
> **1** bed　**2** bee　**3** beat　**4** be
>
> **1** be　**2** he　**3** me　**4** she　**5** we
>
> **1** be　**2** bet　**3** been　**4** beat
> **5** me　**6** men　**7** meet　**8** mean
> **9** he　**10** hen　**11** heel　**12** heat
> **13** she　**14** shed　**15** sheep
> **16** we　**17** when　**18** weep　**19** wheat　**20** wheel
>
> **1** meet　**2** me　**3** met　**4** mean　**5** men　**6** wheat
> **7** wet　**8** we　**9** when　**10** weep　**11** sheet
> **12** shed　**13** she　**14** sea　**15** heap　**16** heel
> **17** hem　**18** he　**19** hen　**20** Ben　**21** been　**22** be
> **23** bee　**24** beach　**25** wheel

Exercise 2: Number from 1–7

Follow the usual procedure.

Answers

Exercise 3: Listen and tick

Follow the usual procedure. Replay (or say again) any difficult pairs if students have difficulty.

Answers

Exercise 4: Trace and write

Remind the students that *h* and *b* are tall letters. Follow the usual procedure.

Exercise 5: Find the different word

Follow the usual procedure.

Answers

be	BE	(he)	be	Be
The	the	the	the	(then)
she	she	she	(sea)	she
we	(Wii)	WE	We	we
he	(HE)	he	(the)	He

Exercise 6: Look

Students read the words silently. Give a number and ask selected students to read out the word.

Exercise 7: Highlight *the* in the text

Including the one already highlighted, there are 12 occurrences of *the*. This is a new activity. Point out that students do not have to understand every word in the text. You could set the activity using photos of Manchester United or a football match. Ask the students to highlight each occurrence of *the*, and to count them. Ask them how many they found. If there is disagreement, ask them to double-check. Check their answers again. Show them the 12 occurences highlighted on an OHT/IWB.

Answers

(The) Manchester United football team are in (the) United Arab Emirates today. They arrived at (the) Dubai International Airport on a British Airways flight, and went to (the) Shangri-La Hotel for lunch. (The) team are playing this evening against (the) national team at (the) Al-Rashid Stadium. (The) match begins at 8 p.m. (The) referee is from (the) People's Republic of China. (The) stadium will be full for the match.

Exercise 8: Read, then listen and check

This exercise demonstrates the spellings of /iː/ in different contexts and practises the pronunciation of *e* in different contexts. It also revises & and @. Comment on the fact that these are extremely high-frequency words. Students will get a sense of achievement and be motivated when they are learning very useful words. Quickly read aloud each item with students following in their books (or use an OHT/IWB). Then set as pairwork. A student gives a number between 1 and 10; their partner reads the corresponding word. Reverse roles. Monitor and correct. Play the CD with students following in their books (or use an OHT/IWB).

Exercise 9: Read the text messages, then listen and check

Ask students to read the first message silently. Students do not have to understand all the words. Ask students to find the names and times in the texts. Play the CD for the first message. Check their pronunciation, including names and times. Work through the other seven text messages in the same way.

Closure

Use flashcards to review the new words learnt in this unit.

19 A Y A I

Objectives
By the end of the lesson, students should be able to:

- read *ai* and terminal *ay* as /eɪ/;
- distinguish between *a* for /æ/ as already learnt, and the new forms of *ai* and terminal *ay*;
- recognize lower-case and capital versions of the new letter combinations;
- read aloud one- and two-syllable words that exemplify the new letter combinations;
- demonstrate recognition of previously learnt letters and words.

Adaptations

Faster/mixed-ability classes	Directed self-study
As this is the first time a diphthong (/eɪ/) has been introduced, together with two spellings of it, start with Exercise 6 as a test. If this is dealt with satisfactorily, go back to Exercise 3 as the beginning. Otherwise, do the whole unit.	As this is the first time a diphthong (/eɪ/) has been introduced, together with two spellings of it, go over the sounds for *ay* and *ai* using Exercise 6. Based on their performance in that exercise, tell student(s) which exercises to do. Remind them that they can replay the CD, or pause it, if they wish.

Words for revision
(also available as flashcards)

be	bee	he	heap	hem	hen	me
sea	she	shed	sheet	we	weep	

New letters/words for this lesson
(also available as flashcards)

ay /eɪ/   ai /eɪ/

aid	aim	bay	chain	day	fail	gay
hail	hay	jail	jay	laid	lay	mail
mailbox	main	nail	pain	pay	rail	railway
rain	ray	sail	say	tail	wail	wait
way						

Introduction

This unit introduces the first diphthong, /eɪ/, together with two spellings of it. Take care to communicate to the students the two elements in the diphthong: /e/+/ɪ/.

Write words from the revision list on the board (or use flashcards or an OHT/IWB). Choose between these activities:
- students listen and repeat selected words
- designated students read out words

Exercise 1: Read and say

This exercise revises *o, a, e, i, u, oo, ee* and *ea*, and contrasts these with the new letter combinations *ay* and *ai*. Ensure you give the right pronunciation of *o, e, i* and *u*. Exploit the visual

to heighten interest. Pronounce the *rail* in *railway* as /r/+/eɪ/+/l/. Follow the normal procedure. When you get to the third section, ask the students to spot the name (*Hal*).

Transcript 2.31 (2 mins, 21 secs)

1 a	**2** ay	**3** ai	**4** AY	**5** AI			
1 o	**2** a	**3** e	**4** i	**5** u	**6** oo	**7** ee	**8** ea	**9** ay
10 ai	**11** a	**12** ea	**13** ai	**14** a	**15** ay	**16** oo	
17 o	**18** u						

1 pan	**2** pain	**3** pay	**4** Hal	**5** hail	**6** hay

1 bay	**2** day	**3** gay	**4** hay	**5** jay	**6** lay	**7** may
8 pay	**9** ray	**10** say	**11** way	**12** aid	**13** chain	
14 fail	**15** jail	**16** laid	**17** mail	**18** main	**19** nail	
20 pain	**21** rail	**22** sail	**23** tail	**24** wait	**25** aim	

Exercise 2: Number from 1–7

Follow the usual procedure.

Answers

Transcript 2.32 (0 mins, 26 secs)

1 wait	**2** rail	**3** pay	**4** day	**5** mail	**6** way	**7** may

Exercise 3: Listen and tick

Follow the usual procedure. Replay (or say again) any difficult pairs if students have difficulty.

Answers

Transcript 🎧 **2.33** (0 mins, 30 secs)

main	way	day	nail	wait
say	may	rain	paid	laid

Exercise 4: Trace and write

Point out the descender on *y* and the ascender on *l*, and remind the students that *d* and *t* are tall letters. Follow the usual procedure.

Exercise 5: Read and label

Follow the usual procedure.

Answers

1 chain   **2** May   **3** mailbox   **4** pay   **5** hay

Exercise 6: Read, say and check

Play the CD, only stopping if necessary. Students follow in their books and repeat each word in the pauses. Try to maintain pace.

Transcript 🎧 **2.34** (1 min, 0 secs)

1 got	**2** soon	**3** wet	**4** we	**5** weep	**6** wheat
7 mad	**8** may	**9** mail	**10** chat	**11** chain	**12** sail
13 say	**14** sack	**15** aim	**16** aid	**17** paid	**18** gain
19 gay	**20** gap	**21** wail	**22** way	**23** rain	

Exercise 7: Read, then listen and check

Students read the words silently. Check they are reading down the columns. Give them 30 seconds to read all the words. Play the CD for feedback.

Transcript 🎧 **2.35** (0 mins, 38 secs)

e-mail	railway	May Day	get paid
mailbox	pay me	payday	pay soon
chat room	way in	wait in	rain hat

Exercise 8: Find and circle all the words with *ay / ai*

Ask students to read and highlight every occurrence of *ai* and *ay* that they can find. Show an OHT/IWB with the occurrences highlighted. Ask students to read back highlighted words.

Answers

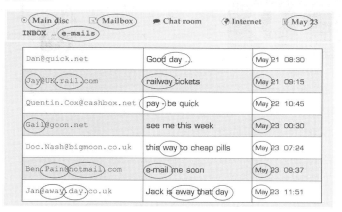

Closure

Return to Exercise 7. Go round the class, getting students to read the words and phrases aloud.

20 N O O A ~ O E .

Objectives
By the end of the lesson, students should be able to:

- read final *o*, *oa* + *consonant* and final *oe* as /əʊ/;
- read and pronounce the vowel in *open*, *don't* and *won't* as /əʊ/;
- read telephone numbers containing 0 (see Unit 1);
- recognize lower-case and capital versions of the new letter combinations;
- read aloud words that contain /əʊ/ written as *o*, *oa* and *oe*;
- demonstrate recognition of previously learnt letters and words.

Adaptations

Faster/mixed-ability classes	Directed self-study
As in previous units, you could start with Exercise 3 as a test, and go back to the earlier exercises only if necessary.	Go over the letter *o* and the letter combinations *oa~* and *oe*, which all represent one sound (/əʊ/) in their respective contexts. Tell student(s) which exercises to do on the basis of their abilities. Remind them that they can replay the CD, or pause it, if they wish.

Words for revision
(also available as flashcards)

aid	aim	bay	chain	day	fail	gay
hail	hay	jail	jay	laid	lay	mail
mailbox	main	nail	pain	pay	rail	railway
rain	ray	sail	say	tail	wail	wait
way						

New letters/words for this lesson
(also available as flashcards)

no /əʊ/   oa~ /əʊ/   oe /əʊ/

boat	coach	coat	doe	don't	foam	foe
goat	Joe	load	loan	moan	oat	open
road	roam	soak	soap	toe	woe	won't

Introduction

Write words from the revision list on the board/IWB (or use flashcards or an OHT). Choose between these activities:
- students listen and repeat selected words
- designated students read out words

Exercise 1: Read and say

Point out that this unit introduces three ways of writing a single diphthong (/əʊ/), according to context. Students may need help with this – break it down into its two component sounds and build up. Exploit the visual to heighten interest.

Draw attention to the pronunciation of *open*. Follow the normal procedure.

Exercise 2: Number from 1–7

Follow the usual procedure.

Answers

Exercise 3: Listen and tick

Point out that *a pen* is two words. Follow the usual procedure. Replay (or say again) any difficult pairs if students have difficulty.

goat	moan	rod	roam	coat
coach	doe	open	so	got

Exercise 4: Trace and write

Point out the descender on *g* and remind the students that *d* and *t* are tall letters. Follow the usual procedure.

Exercise 5: Read and label

Follow the usual procedure.

Answers

1 boat **2** soap **3** coach **4** coat **5** goat

Exercise 6: Read and say

This exercise is broken down into two sections. For items 1–11 in the second section, students read the words with a partner. Monitor, but do not confirm or correct. Play the CD. Elicit the correct pronunciation of each word. Play the CD again, if necessary.

01-202-3456   020-709-0430

1 no **2** do **3** don't **4** open **5** woe **6** won't
7 the **8** open **9** you **10** don't **11** won't

Exercise 7: Read, then listen and check.

With a partner, students read the phrases. Make sure they are reading down the columns. Monitor, but do not confirm or correct. Play the CD. Elicit the correct pronunciation of each word. Play the CD again, if necessary. The pictures are just for illustration but could be incorporated into the exercise. Taking turns, students point to a picture and their partner reads it. Monitor and correct.

No way!	no soap	big toe	won't go
Go this way	no coat	don't eat that	won't get
soap dish	no road	don't go	won't say
hand soap	no coach	don't say no	won't see

Exercise 8: Find words from Unit 20

Use this exercise for the Closure. Follow the usual procedure.

Answers

Closure

Use Exercise 8 as the Closure.

21 A R

Objectives

By the end of the lesson, students should be able to:

- recognize and read initial *ar + consonant* or *consonant + ar* + consonant as /ɑː/;
- distinguish between /ɑː/ and /æ/ (when *a + other consonant* (not *r*));
- demonstrate recognition of previously learnt letters and words.

Adaptations

Faster/mixed-ability classes	Directed self-study
As in previous units, you could start with Exercise 3 as a test, and go back to the earlier exercises only if necessary.	Go over the letters *a* and *r*, which have the vowel sound /ɑː/. Tell student(s) which exercises to do. Remind them that they can replay the CD, or pause it, if they wish.

Words for revision
(also available as flashcards)

boat	coach	coat	doe	don't	foam	foe
goat	Joe	load	moan	oat	open	road
roam	soak	soap	toe	woe	won't	

New letters/words for this lesson
(also available as flashcards)

ar /ɑː/

arc	arm	art	bar	bard	bark	car
card	charm	chart	dark	far	farm	hard
harm	jar	lark	mark	park	part	tart

Introduction

Write words from the revision list on the board/IWB (or use flashcards or an OHT). Choose between these activities:
- **students listen and repeat selected words**
- **designated students read out words**

Exercise 1: Read and say

This exercise introduces *ar* (essentially a way of writing /ɑː/). It contrasts this letter combination with other *vowel + consonant* combinations previously learnt, where both the vowel and the consonant are pronounced. Exploit the visual to heighten interest. Read it to the class. Follow the normal procedure, monitoring to ensure students pronounce *ar* as the open vowel /ɑː/.

Pronunciation note

The target pronunciation here is British RP, which does not pronounce *r* before a consonant or at the end of a word (when *r* is pronounced in these contexts, it is called rhotic *r*).

Transcript 🔊 2.41 (1 min, 42 secs)

1 a	2 ai	3 ay	4 ar	5 o	6 oo	7 e	8 ee	9 ea
10 oa	11 oe	12 ar						

1 cat	2 car	3 fan	4 far	5 am	6 arm	7 pat
8 part						

1 bar	2 car	3 far	4 jar	5 arc	6 arm	7 art

1 bark	2 card	3 charm	4 chart	5 dark	6 farm
7 harm	8 hard	9 bard	10 lark	11 mark	
12 park	13 part	14 tart			

Exercise 2: Number from 1–7

Follow the usual procedure.

Answers

Transcript 🔊 2.42 (0 mins, 25 secs)

1 car	2 cart	3 park	4 far	5 art	6 arm	7 farm

Exercise 3: Listen and tick

Follow the usual procedure. Replay (or say again) any difficult pairs if students have difficulty.

Answers

Transcript 🔊 2.43 (0 mins, 33 secs)

chat	bard	park	lack	hard	jar
dark	harm	card	far	part	arc

Exercise 4: Trace and write

Point out the descender on *p* and remind the students that *f* and *k* have an ascender. Follow the usual procedure. Then ask students to write out the notice and read it aloud.

Exercise 5: Read and label

Follow the usual procedure.

Answers

1 car **2** jar **3** arm **4** cart **5** card

Exercise 6: Match the words to the signs

This is a silent reading activity. Students join matching phrases and pictures with an arrow, then check each other's solutions.

Exercise 7: Separate the words

Follow the usual procedure. Allow time in the lesson planning for slow writers. Give out sheets of paper for poor writers, as they tend to have large writing.

Answers

hard / mark / dark / lark
farm / harm / charm / tart
jar / arm / art / part / arc
beach / road / car / park

Exercise 8: Read the key words at speed

Note that meaning is not important in this exercise, but if students do know the words, it will help their English. They are mainly *grammatical* words which have very high frequency – hence they are key words. Play the CD, only stopping if necessary. As this is a *reading* exercise (not a *listening* exercise), students should follow in their books and repeat each word in the pauses. Try to maintain pace.

Transcript 2.44 (1 min, 30 secs)

a	am	an	and	&	at	@	be	been	bit
but	can	day	did	do	don't	each	eat	get
go	got	had	he	him	if	in	it	let	lot
may	me	mean	much	no	not	on	read
room	say	see	seen	she	shop	so	soon
than	that	the	them	this	too	up	us	we
when	which	with	won't	yes	you

Exercise 9: Read, then listen and check

Play the CD. Then ask students to read down the columns. Students take it in turns to read each phrase. Monitor, but do not correct. Practise pronunciation with the whole class. As a final phase, replay the CD with students following in their books.

Transcript 2.45 (0 min, 58 secs)

car park	red card	part six	beach car park
coach park	art card	ten marks	sheep farm
pay and park	coffee bar	top mark	goat farm
bad arm	tea bar	jam jar	dark day

Exercise 10: Dictation

The dictation is on the CD, but you may prefer to read it aloud yourself. It is the first dictation in the course, so make sure students know what to do. This is a consolidation of the learning in the unit, not a test. Give plenty of time for students to write down the answers and repeat a word, if necessary. The objective is success. When finished, ask individual students to read back each item, which you then write on the board or show on a flashcard.

Answers

Transcript 2.46 (0 mins, 38 secs)

| **1** park | **2** pack | **3** farm | **4** jar | **5** part |

Closure

Use Exercise 7 as the Closure. To correct and provide feedback, firstly ask how many words there are in each row, and then read them out yourself. Who was right about the number of words?

22  S T ~ ~ S T

Objectives

By the end of the lesson, students should be able to:

- recognize and read *st~* and *st~*;
- demonstrate recognition of previously learnt letters and words.

Adaptations

Faster/mixed-ability classes	Directed self-study
As in previous units, you could start with Exercise 3 as a test, and go back to the earlier exercises only if necessary.	Go over the consonant cluster *st*. Tell student(s) which exercises to do. Remind them that they can replay the CD, or pause it, if they wish.

Notes on new sounds

This is the first time that students have encountered a consonant cluster, as opposed to two letters representing one sound. When modelling *st* for students, avoid finishing with a vowel sound. When *st* starts a word, speakers of some languages precede *s* (/s/) with a vowel. Monitor this and correct. Similarly, consonant clusters are not possible in some languages and speakers of these languages will tend to separate *s* and *t* with a vowel sound.

Words for revision
(also available as flashcards)

arc	arm	art	bar	bark	car	card
charm	chart	dark	far	farm	hard	harm
jar	lark	mark	park	part	tart	

New letters/words for this lesson
(also available as flashcards)

st /st/

beast	best	boast	bust	chest	coast	cost
dust	east	feast	fist	just	least	list
lost	must	quest	rest	roast	rust	stab
stack	stain	star	start	stash	stay	steal
steam	steel	stem	stick	stock	stool	stop
stuck	stun	test	toast	vest	waist	west

Introduction

This is the first time two letters have been introduced to spell a *spoken* consonant cluster (*st*). The two-letter combination *ck*, introduced earlier, spelt *one* spoken sound (/k/). Write words from the revision list on the board/IWB (or use flashcards or an OHT). Choose between these activities:

- **students listen and repeat selected words**
- **designated students read out words**

Exercise 1: Read and say

This exercise introduces *st*. In the first section, note how *st* is preceded by *s* and *t* separately. See *Notes on new sounds* above for possible problems. Exploit the visual to heighten interest. Read it to the class. Then follow the normal procedure.

Transcript 🎵 **2.47** (2 mins, 47 secs)

1 s **2** t **3** st **4** b **5** ch **6** sh **7** s **8** ck **9** qu **10** st

1 star **2** start **3** stay **4** best **5** just **6** must

1 stab **2** stack **3** stash **4** star **5** start **6** stain
7 stay **8** steal **9** steam **10** steel **11** stem
12 stick **13** stock **14** stop **15** stool **16** stuck
17 stun

1 east **2** best **3** rest **4** test **5** vest **6** west
7 chest **8** fist **9** list **10** cost **11** lost **12** bust
13 dust **14** just **15** must **16** rust **17** beast
18 feast **19** least **20** boast **21** coast **22** roast
23 toast **24** waist

Exercise 2: Number from 1–7

Follow the usual procedure.

Answers

Transcript 🎵 **2.48** (0 mins, 49 secs)

1 stick **2** star **3** stun **4** stool **5** steam **6** stop
7 stay

1 east **2** toast **3** best **4** waist **5** list **6** lost
7 just

Exercise 3: Listen and tick

Follow the usual procedure. Replay (or say again) any difficult pairs if students have difficulty.

Answers

Transcript 2.49 (0 mins, 42 secs)

stab	top	stick	tool	steal	stock	sack
east	vest	fit	boast	waist	lost	wet

Exercise 4: Trace and write

At this stage, it is probably no longer necessary to point out the descenders, ascenders and other features. However, check to see if any students have problems. Follow the usual procedure.

Exercise 5: Read, say and check

Break the exercise down into three stages, taking eight items at a time. Students read words 1–8 silently. Ask students to read out words 1–8. Play the CD for words 1–8 with students listening. Do the same with words 9–16 and 17–24.

Transcript 2.50 (1 min, 6 secs)

1 east	**2** steam	**3** stem	**4** west	**5** coast	**6** stock
7 stun	**8** must	**9** stuck	**10** just	**11** lost	**12** stop
13 toast	**14** stool	**15** least	**16** steal	**17** waist	
18 stay	**19** chest	**20** start	**21** bust	**22** boast	
23 nest	**24** quest				

Exercise 6: Read, then listen and check

Tell the students to read down the columns, not across the page. Students read the words silently. Play the CD, with students listening to each word. Allow time at each stage because the students may still be slow readers.

Transcript 2.51 (0 mins, 55 secs)

the best way	rock star	stop and start
east to west	moon and stars	coast road
The Far East	sun, moon and stars	the east coast
The Far West	see the sun, moon and stars	the west coast

Exercise 7: Complete the sentences with the words in the box

This is comparatively difficult, as students have to understand the meaning of the sentences to get the answer. However, the sentences and the vocabulary are basic and unlikely to be too difficult. Initially, this exercise can be done orally, guiding students to the meaning of the sentences to enable them to select the missing word. The oral approach also involves the whole class in the process of discovery. Exploit the visuals to elucidate meanings. After the oral phase, students can write down the answers. Give out sheets of paper to writers who still find small writing hard to do.

Answers

1 east   **2** west   **3** start   **4** star

Exercise 8: Read the words on the sat nav map

Students work with a partner. One student points to words and their partner reads them. Reverse roles.

Exercise 9: Find the different word

Follow the normal procedure.

Answers

best	best	BEST	beat
must	must	just	must
start	star	start	start
toast	toast	boast	toast

Closure

Tell students to learn the meanings of the following words from today's lesson: *toast, steam, steel, rust, dust, stick, chest* and *waist*.

Objectives

By the end of the lesson, students should be able to:

- recognize and read *cr~* and *tr~* in lower-case and capitals in words of one syllable and more;

- demonstrate recognition of previously learnt letters, letter combinations and words.

Adaptations

Faster/mixed-ability classes	Directed self-study
You could start with Exercise 6 as a test, and go back to Exercise 3 or Exercise 1 according to students' performance.	Briefly revise the consonant cluster *ck* and vowel sounds spelt with two letters: *ea*, *ee* and *ai*. Go over the new two-letter combinations and sounds. Tell student(s) which exercises to do. Remind them that they can replay the CD, or pause it, if they wish.

Words for revision

(also available as flashcards)

beast	best	boast	bust	chest	coast	cost
dust	east	feast	fist	just	least	list
lost	must	rest	roast	rust	stab	stack
stain	star	start	stash	stay	steam	steel
stem	stick	toast	stock	stool	stop	stuck
stun	test	vest	waist	west		

New letters/words for this lesson

(also available as flashcards)

cr /kr/   tr /tr/

crack	cram	crash	cream	credit	creep
crest	crick	crop	cross	crossroads	crush
crust	crutch	track	trail	train	tram
trap	trash	travel	tray	treat	tree
trek	trick	troop	trot	truck	trust

Introduction

Write words from the revision list on the board/IWB (or use flashcards or an OHT). Choose between these activities:
- **students listen and repeat selected words**
- **individual designated students read out words**

Exercise 1: Read and say

Exploit the visual to heighten interest. Read it to the class. Follow the normal procedure, but monitor carefully and do not allow students to insert a vowel sound between the two consonants.

Transcript ◉ 2.52 (1 min, 55 secs)

1 k   **2** r   **3** cr   **4** t   **5** r   **6** tr

1 cash   **2** crash   **3** tap   **4** trap

1 crack   **2** crash   **3** cream   **4** creep   **5** crest
6 crick   **7** cross   **8** crop   **9** crust   **10** crutch
11 crush   **12** credit

1 tram   **2** trap   **3** track   **4** trail   **5** train   **6** trash
7 tray   **8** trek   **9** tree   **10** treat   **11** trick   **12** trip
13 trot   **14** troop   **15** truck   **16** trust   **17** travel

Exercise 2: Number from 1–7

Follow the usual procedure.

Answers

Transcript ◉ 2.53 (0 mins, 42 secs)

1 cross   **2** cream   **3** crutch   **4** crick   **5** crust
6 crash   **7** credit

1 trot   **2** troop   **3** trek   **4** tree   **5** trap   **6** truck
7 trip

Exercise 3: Listen and tick

Follow the usual procedure. Replay (or say again) any difficult pairs if students have difficulty.

Answers

Transcript ◉ 2.54 (0 mins, 39 secs)

rap   tree   truck   tick   trick   train   trash

rush   crash   rack   cross   crash   cram   crush

Exercise 4: Trace and write

None of the letters in this unit is new and it is probably no longer necessary to point out the ascenders and other features. However, check to see if any students have problems. Follow the usual procedure.

Exercise 5: Read and label

Follow the usual procedure.

Answers

1 train   **2** truck   **3** crossroads   **4** tram   **5** credit card

Exercise 6: Read the key words at speed

This exercise exclusively revises letters/sounds from earlier units. Play the CD, only stopping if necessary. As this is a *reading* exercise (not a *listening* exercise), students should follow in their books and repeat each word in the pauses. Try to maintain pace. If the students find the task too difficult, leave it for now and return to it another time.

> **Transcript** 🎵 2.55 (1 min, 33 secs)
>
> a   am   an   and   &   at   @   be   been   bit but   can   day   did   do   don't   each   eat   get go   got   had   he   him   if   in   it   just   let lot   may   me   mean   much   must   no   not on   read   room   say   see   seen   she   shop   so soon   than   that   the   them   this   too   up   us we   when   which   with   won't   yes   you

Exercise 7: Read, then listen and check

Students read the phrases silently. Remind students they do not need to understand every word. However, you can remind students of the meanings of *train*, *truck* and *tram* from Exercise 5. Play the CD with students listening to each phrase. Allow time at each stage because the students may still be slow readers.

> **Transcript** 🎵 2.56 (1 min, 25 secs)
>
> a train   a railway train   track   on a track   a railway train on a track
>
> trash   a trash can   a crack   a crack in a trash can
>
> crash   truck   a truck crash   into a tree   a truck crash into a tree
>
> credit card   trust a credit card   can we trust a credit card?
>
> a tram   a tram at a crossroads   a tram on tracks at a crossroads
>
> a tray   a tray of toast and jam and coffee and cream in a cup

Exercise 8: Read and copy

If possible, bring in one or two receipts to show students. Ask them if they have any in their pockets or wallets. Exploit the visual of the receipt as far as possible; two of the words here have been taught using pictures (*crossroads*, *credit card*). If necessary, refer students back to the relevant visuals. Ask the students simply to fill in the missing letters. Then either go round the class, monitoring and correcting where necessary, or the students work individually and then with a partner, correcting each other's work.

Exercise 9: Find words from Unit 23

Use this exercise as the Closure. Follow the usual procedure.

Answers

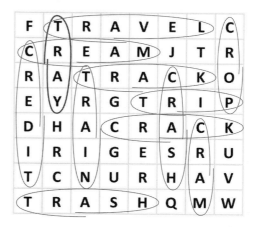

Closure

Use Exercise 9 as the Closure.

24 · B R · D R · F R · G R · P R

Objectives

By the end of the lesson, students should be able to:

- recognize and read *br~*, *dr~*, *fr~*, *gr~* and *pr~* in lower case and capitals, in words of one syllable and more;

- demonstrate recognition of previously learnt letters, letter combinations and words.

Adaptations

Faster/mixed-ability classes	Directed self-study
As in previous units, you could start with Exercise 2 as a test, and go back to Exercise 1 only if necessary.	There are some new exercise types in this lesson (4, 5, 6) so make sure you explain these carefully and check understanding.
	Go over the consonant letters/sounds. Tell student(s) which exercises to do. Remind them that they can replay the CD, or pause it, if they wish.
	If possible, do the first three sections of Exercise 1 with the students before they do self-study. Check that they are discriminating between all the consonant clusters.

Words for revision
(also available as flashcards)

crack	cram	crash	cream	credit	creep
crest	crick	crop	cross	crossroads	crush
crust	crutch	track	trail	train	tram
trap	trash	travel	tray	treat	tree
trek	trick	troop	trot	truck	trust

New letters/words for this lesson
(also available as flashcards)

br /br/ dr /dr/ fr /fr/ gr /gr/ pr /pr/

afraid	agree	brain	bran	brash	breed	brick
broom	brush	drag	drain	dream	drip	drop
drum	frail	freak	free	fresh	frock	frog
from	frost	grab	gram	grand	green	greet
grin	grip	grub	pram	pray	prick	proof
prop						

Introduction

Write words from the revision list on the board/IWB (or use flashcards or an OHT). Choose between these activities:

- **students listen and repeat selected words**
- **designated students read out words**

Exercise 1: Read and say

Exploit the visual. Follow the normal procedure but, as in Unit 23, make sure that students are not inserting a vowel between the two consonants.

Transcript 🔊 **2.57** (3 mins, 32 secs)

1 br **2** cr **3** dr **4** fr **5** gr **6** pr **7** tr

1 b **2** br **3** d **4** dr **5** f **6** fr **7** g **8** gr **9** p **10** pr

1 rain **2** brain **3** rip **4** drip **5** rail **6** frail **7** ram **8** gram **9** ray **10** pray

1 bran **2** brain **3** brash **4** breed **5** brick **6** broom **7** brush **8** drag **9** drain **10** dream **11** drop **12** drip **13** drum

1 frail **2** free **3** fresh **4** freak **5** from **6** frost **7** grab **8** gram **9** grand **10** green **11** greet **12** grin **13** grip **14** grub **15** pram **16** pray **17** prop **18** proof **19** agree **20** afraid

1 dream **2** cream **3** greet **4** grand **5** fresh **6** frost **7** pay **8** pray **9** gram **10** gain **11** grain **12** brush **13** brash **14** frail **15** afraid **16** green **17** agree **18** drain **19** brain **20** pain **21** proof **22** grub **23** grab **24** drum **25** frock **26** from **27** frog

Exercise 2: Listen and tick

Follow the usual procedure. Replay (or say again) any difficult pairs if students have difficulty.

Answers

Transcript ● 2.58 (0 mins, 41 secs)

brain	brush	drip	dip	free	frog	grub	gain
pram	roof	afraid	agreed	drain	bash	brick	
bran							

Exercise 3: Trace and write

None of the letters in this unit are new, only the combinations. It is probably no longer necessary to point out the descenders, ascenders and other features. However, check to see if any students have problems. Follow the usual procedure.

Exercise 4: Find and circle the words with *cr / br / dr / fr / gr / pr / tr*

Students should do this individually. Allow two minutes. Monitor. Then, with a partner, students can check each other's work. Feed back the answers using an OHT/IWB with the words circled. There are no words containing *dr*.

Answers

Exercise 5: Find words with the same sound

An example has been provided. Ask students to complete individually. Then ask individual students to volunteer to read out each pair of words.

Answers

pray – tray; free – agree; gram – pram; brain – drain; grand – hand; drop – prop; dream – cream; grab – drab.

Exercise 6: Add the key words, then listen and check

This is a test of relating what is read to the sound it represents. In this case, a different vowel is being tested in each line. Each word in a line has the same vowel. This is a new activity, so set it up carefully. From the grey box, students must select the word that has the same vowel sound. Students could work individually or with a partner. Allow three minutes maximum. Then play the CD. At the end of each

recorded line, stop the CD and ask designated students to complete the line with the right word from the list.

Transcript ● 2.59 (1 min, 13 secs)

be	been	each	eat	he	me	mean	read
see	seen	she	**we**			
bit	did	him	if	in	this	which	**with**
am	an	at	can	had	than	**that**
don't	go	no	so	**won't**		
day	may	**say**				
do	**you**					

Exercise 7: Read, then listen and check

Tell students to read down the columns. Students read the phrases silently. Play the CD, with students listening to each phrase.

Transcript ● 2.60 (0 mins, 43 secs)

drag and drop	free tea	ten grams
drumstick	greet me	six grams
brain drain	drop in trash	agree with me
brush and broom	grab, drag and drop	he is afraid

Exercise 8: Dictation

The dictation is on the CD, but you may prefer to read it yourself. Make sure everyone knows what to do. Remember that this dictation is not a test, but a consolidation of the learning in the unit. Therefore: read naturally, give plenty of time for everyone to write down the answers and repeat a word if necessary. The objective is success. When finished, ask individual students to read back each word, which you then write on the board or show on a flashcard.

Answers

Transcript ● 2.61 (0 mins, 35 secs)

1 drag   **2** grab   **3** gram   **4** afraid   **5** pray

Closure

Put these words from the unit on the board (or OHT): *brain, brush, cross, dream, fresh, greet, grin* and *track*. Ask students to underline them in the Course Book. This in itself is a reading exercise. Ask them to learn the words before beginning the next unit.

25

Objectives
By the end of the lesson, students should be able to:

■ associate sight and sound of the letters *a~e* (as in *mate*) as capitals and lower case, in a variety of typefaces;

■ distinguish *a~e* from *a~* (as in *mat*);

■ demonstrate understanding that the diphthong /eɪ/ can be written three different ways;

■ demonstrate understanding that how /eɪ/ is spelt is fixed for any given word;

■ recognize and produce previously learnt letters, letter combinations and words.

Adaptations

Faster/mixed-ability classes	Directed self-study
Allow enough time for the more challenging later activities, e.g., Exercises 5 and 6. You could start with Exercise 2 as a test, and go back to Exercise 1 only if necessary.	Go over the new letter pattern/sound, ensuring students grasp the vowel change from /æ/ to /eɪ/ when final e is added. Check students understand Exercises 5 and 6. Tell student(s) which exercises to do. Remind them that they can replay the CD, or pause it, if they wish.

Notes on new sounds
The diphthong /eɪ/ is not new, only this way of writing it. The last single vowel in a word is lengthened by adding a final *e*. Point out that the vowel sound /eɪ/ is identical in *sale* and *sail*, for example.

Words for revision
(also available as flashcards)

agree	afraid	brain	bran	brash	breed	brick
broom	brush	drag	drain	dream	drip	drop
drum	frail	freak	free	fresh	frock	frog
from	frost	grab	gram	grand	green	greet
grin	grip	grub	pram	pray	prick	proof
prop						

New letters/words for this lesson
(also available as flashcards)

a~e /eɪ/

base	brake	brave	cake	cane	case	cave
dam	dame	date	fame	fate	frame	game
gate	gave	grape	grate	grave	hate	Kate
lack	lake	lane	late	laze	mad	made
maid	mane	mate	maze	name	rave	safe
sail	sake	sale	same	shack	shake	shape
shave	state	take	tape	wake	wave	whale

Introduction
Write words from the revision list on the board/IWB (or use flashcards or an OHT). Choose between these activities:
- **students listen and repeat selected words**
- **designated students read out words**

Exercise 1: Read and say
Exploit the visual. Demonstrate the vowel change from /æ/ to /eɪ/ when final *e* is added. As there are so many words in each section, make sure you vary the procedure you use for different sections. For example:
- Sections 1–2: Listen and repeat. Play the CD. Students listen and repeat.
- Section 3:
  - Words 1–15: Listen and say the *a~e* words. Use the numbers to elicit the words containing *final consonant + e* already encountered (*3 came, 6 dame, 11 made, 16 sale, 19 tape*).
  - Words 16–26: Read and say. Use the numbers to elicit the words. Do not confirm or correct. Play the CD. Ask students to read the words again by pointing to different words on an OHT/IWB.
- Section 4:
  - Pairwork: Student A says a number; Student B says the corresponding word. Monitor. Play the CD for students to compare their answers.

- Delayed oral production: Students simply listen to the CD. Having listened to all the words, students move on to Exercise 2.
- Listen and point: Say a word at random from the row. Students point to the correct word.

Transcript 3.1 (2 mins, 51 secs)

1 mad	**2** may	**3** maid	**4** made	**5** Sal	**6** say
7 sail	**8** sale				

1 mad	**2** made	**3** tap	**4** tape	**5** hat	**6** hate
7 can	**8** cane	**9** dam	**10** dame		

1 brake	**2** cake	**3** came	**4** cane	**5** case	**6** dame
7 date	**8** fate	**9** game	**10** late	**11** made	
12 make	**13** name	**14** rave	**15** safe	**16** sale	
17 same	**18** take	**19** tape	**20** wake	**21** shake	
22 shave	**23** state	**24** brave	**25** grave	**26** whale	

1 came	**2** same	**3** fame	**4** name	**5** game	**6** hate
7 late	**8** state	**9** date	**10** gate	**11** mate	**12** lake
13 brake	**14** cake	**15** shake	**16** wake	**17** brave	
18 shave	**19** cave	**20** grape	**21** wave	**22** case	
23 maze	**24** tape	**25** frame	**26** shape		

Exercise 2: Listen and tick

Follow the usual procedure. Replay (or say again) any difficult pairs if students have difficulty.

Answers

Transcript 3.2 (0 mins, 37 secs)

brake	mat	gave	can	same	shake	save
frame	base	late	maze	sale	fat	name

Exercise 3: Trace and write

Follow the usual procedure.

Exercise 4: Read and label

Follow the usual procedure.

Answers

1 cake   **2** date   **3** grapes   **4** gate   **5** case

Exercise 5: Tick (✓) the same sounds and cross (✗) the different sounds

Using the example to explain, emphasize that it is the vowel sound (not the consonants) that the students must judge as the same, or different, in each pair. Students should do this individually. Allow two minutes. Monitor. Students check each other's work with a partner. Feed back the answers using an OHT/IWB with pairs of words ticked or crossed.

Answers

1 ✓   **2** ✗   **3** ✗   **4** ✓   **5** ✗   **6** ✓   **7** ✓   **8** ✗

Exercise 6: Find and circle the words with *ay / ai*

Students complete this individually and then compare their answers with a partner. Use an OHT/IWB to show the right answers.

Answers

Exercise 7: Read, say and check

Students read items silently. They choose by number a word for their partner to read out. Then reverse roles. Allow three minutes for this – enough time for each student to have read a large proportion of the 24 words to their partner. Monitor and correct. Play the CD, with students listening to each word. If you think it necessary, ask students to repeat each item while reading in their books.

Transcript 3.3 (1 min, 1 sec)

1 sat	**2** state	**3** cat	**4** Kate	**5** lack	**6** lake
7 shack	**8** shake	**9** hate	**10** hat	**11** hay	**12** mat
13 may	**14** mate	**15** greet	**16** grate	**17** mean	
18 save	**19** shape	**20** fat	**21** frame	**22** fate	
23 name	**24** whale				

Exercise 8: Read, then listen and check

Tell students to read down the columns. Follow the usual procedure.

Transcript 3.4 (0 mins, 58 secs)

man-made	same day	car brake	bake a cake
late train	farm gate	main name	make tea
wake up	brush shave	same date	shake and wave
brave man	sea wave	Sam came	made from this

Exercise 9: Dictation

Follow the procedure described in Unit 24, Exercise 8.

Answers

Transcript 3.5 (0 mins, 32 secs)

1 wave	**2** shake	**3** brake	**4** made	**5** date

Closure

Go back to the OHT/IWB for Exercise 5. Point to different words and ask students to read them. This will revise and consolidate what they have learnt. Ask students to learn the meaning of these words: *cake, brake, brave, date, gate, shake, wake* and *wave*.

26   I ~ E

Objectives

By the end of the lesson, students should be able to:

- associate sight and sound of the letters *i~e* (as in *kite*) as capitals and lower case, in a variety of typefaces;
- distinguish *i~e* from *i~* (as in *kit*);
- demonstrate they can read *I('m)* as /aɪ/(m)/;
- recognize and read spelt-out versions of 3, 5, 7, 9 and 10;
- demonstrate recognition and production of previously learnt letters, letter combinations and words.

Adaptations

Faster/mixed-ability classes	Directed self-study
You could start with Exercise 2 as a test, and go back to Exercise 1 only if necessary.	Go over the new letter pattern/sound by doing the first section of Exercise 1 as a group activity. Ensure students grasp the vowel change from /ɪ/ to /aɪ/ when *e* is added. Tell student(s) which exercises to do. Remind them that they can replay the CD, or pause it, if they wish.

Notes on new sounds

Writing and reading the diphthong /aɪ/ is new. You could draw a parallel with *a~e* in Unit 25, where the addition of final *e* also lengthens the last single vowel.

Words for revision
(also available as flashcards)

base	brake	brave	cake	cane	case	cave
dam	dame	date	fame	fate	frame	game
gate	gave	grape	grate	grave	hate	Kate
lack	lake	lane	late	laze	mad	made
maid	mane	mate	maze	name	rave	safe
sail	sake	Sal	sale	Sam	same	shack
shake	shape	shave	state	take	tape	wake
wave	whale					

New letters/words for this lesson
(also available as flashcards)

i~e /aɪ/

bike	bribe	bride	chime	crime	dim	dime
dine	drive	file	fin	fine	five	hike
I	I'm	lick	life	like	lime	Lin
line	mile	mine	nine	pip	pipe	pipeline
quit	quite	ride	shine	Sid	side	sit
site	tide	Tim	time	tribe	while	white
wide	wife					

Introduction

Write words from the revision list on the board/IWB (or use flashcards or an OHT). Choose between these activities:
- **students listen and repeat selected words**
- **designated students read out words**

Exercise 1: Read and say

Exploit the visual. Demonstrate the vowel change from /ɪ/ to /aɪ/ when final *e* is added. Draw students' attention to the words *I* and *I'm* that follow the plus (+) sign in the second section. They are two important words containing the target vowel of the unit, but they are spelt in an exceptional way. As the exercise is long, vary the procedure for the different sections. See Unit 25, Exercise 1 for suggested procedures.

1 pip	**2** pipe	**3** dim	**4** dime	**5** lick	**6** like	**7** fin
8 fine	**9** quit	**10** quite				

1 Sid	**2** side	**3** Tim	**4** time	**5** sit	**6** site	**7** I
8 I'm						

1 bike	**2** chime	**3** crime	**4** dine	**5** file	**6** fine
7 five	**8** life	**9** like	**10** lime	**11** line	**12** mile
13 mine	**14** nine	**15** ride	**16** side	**17** tide	
18 time	**19** wide	**20** wife	**21** shine	**22** drive	
23 bride	**24** tribe	**25** while	**26** white	**27** I'm	

1 ride	**2** mine	**3** hike	**4** quite	**5** like	**6** while
7 fine	**8** white	**9** five	**10** bribe	**11** nine	
12 shine	**13** drive	**14** wife	**15** crime	**16** life	
17 time	**18** file	**19** I'm	**20** chime	**21** wide	
22 pipe	**23** line	**24** pipeline			

3 three	5 five	7 seven	9 nine	10 ten

Exercise 2: Listen and tick

Follow the usual procedure. Replay (or say again) any difficult pairs if students have difficulty.

Answers

made	can	hate	pipe	Tim	quite	lick
site	bit	white	rate	dime	dam	line

Exercise 3: Trace and write

None of the letters in this unit are new, only the combinations. However, reject any spelling of *I* as *i*, as it must be a capital letter – this includes *I'm*. Check to see if any students have problems with this. Follow the usual procedure.

Exercise 4: Complete the sentences

Ask students to work out the missing number for each picture orally. Then complete the sentences by filling in the missing numbers. Write the number, not the word for the number.

Answers

1 3   **2** 7   **3** 5   **4** 10   **5** 9

Exercise 5: Tick (✓) the same sounds and cross (✗) the different sounds

Use the procedure suggested in Unit 25, Exercise 5 for this activity.

Answers

1 ✗   **2** ✓   **3** ✓   **4** ✗   **5** ✗   **6** ✓   **7** ✓   **8** ✗   **9** ✗
10 ✓   **11** ✗   **12** ✓

Exercise 6: Read the names

Students read the names silently for one minute. As the names that end in ~s may cause uncertainty, play the CD first. Point out the pronunciation of *James*, *Miles* and *Niles*. They are just like plurals. Using an OHT/IWB, point to a name and the students read it out, or use flashcards to elicit the names from the students as a group. Repeat either method, asking individual students to respond. Students choose a name for their partner to read out. Then reverse roles. Allow two minutes for this. Monitor and correct as the students work. Play the CD with students listening to each name.

Mick	Mike	Jack	Jake	Nick	Sam	James	Jim
Jo	Jeff	Jan	Jane	Tom	Tim	Kate	Nat	Jade
Dan	Stan	Rick	Miles	Niles			

Exercise 7: Read the sentences

Allow time for the students to scan the sentences to familiarize themselves with them. Using an OHT/IWB, ask the students to name the girl, and then the man. Practise *China* and *Canada*, as the pronunciation of *China* is not obvious from the spelling, and *Canada* – although less problematic – needs confirming for the students. Get students to repeat the sentences as a class, before inviting individual students to read one sentence each. Use the OHT/IWB to indicate what you want them to read.

Hi, I'm Kate. I'm from China.
Hi, I'm Jake. I'm from Canada.

Exercise 8: Read, then listen and check

Follow the usual procedure. For the second section, make sure students are reading down the columns.

Hi, I'm Jan. / Hi, I'm Jane.
I'm not from China.
Hi, I'm Mick. / Hi, I'm Mike.
I'm not from Canada.

lifeline	I like Mike	Is it mine?
pipeline	We like Jane	Is it on time?
five bikes	I don't like Nick	Is it Mike?
a wide lake	Mike likes him	Am I from China?

Exercise 9: Dictation

Follow the usual procedure (see Unit 24, Exercise 8).

Answers

1 pipe	**2** like	**3** while	**4** quite	**5** China

Closure

Put these words from the unit on the board (or OHT): *bike, bite, crime, line, ripe, shine, site* and *wide*. Ask students to underline them in the Course Book. This is a reading exercise in itself. Ask students to learn the meaning of them before beginning the next unit.

27 | O ~ E

Objectives
By the end of the lesson, students should be able to:

■ associate sight and sound of the letters *o~e* (as in *hope*) as capitals and lower case, in a variety of typefaces;

■ distinguish this from *o~* (as in *hop*);

■ recognize and produce previously learnt letters, letter combinations and words.

Adaptations

Faster/mixed-ability classes	Directed self-study
To check ability, ask students (at random) to read out the first section of Exercise 1. Make sure the students observe the vowel change from /ɒ/ to /əʊ/ when ~e is added. If this is satisfactory, move to section four and do the same. Then complete the unit by doing Exercise 3.	Go over the new letter pattern/sounds. Demonstrate the vowel change from /ɒ/ to /əʊ/ when ~e is added. Tell student(s) which exercises to do. Remind them that they can replay the CD, or pause it, if they wish.

Notes on new sounds
Writing and reading the diphthong /əʊ/ is familiar in the form *oa~* and *oe,* when at the end of a word. You could draw a parallel with the introduction of the new spellings *a~e* and *i~e* in Units 25 and 26, where *e* also lengthens the vowel.

Words for revision
(also available as flashcards)

bike	bribe	bride	chime	crime	dim	dime
dine	drive	file	fin	fine	five	hike
I	I'm	lick	life	like	lime	Lin
line	mile	mine	nine	pip	pipe	pipeline
quit	quite	ride	shine	Sid	side	sit
site	tide	Tim	time	tribe	while	white
wide	wife					

New letters/words for this lesson
(also available as flashcards)

o~e /əʊ/

boat	bone	broke	cod	code	cone	cope
cove	drove	hoe	home	hop	hope	hot
hotel	joke	lone	motel	note	pop	pope
probe	rob	robe	rod	rode	rope	stone
stove	tone	vote	weak	wick	woke	zone

Introduction
Write words from the revision list on the board/IWB (or use flashcards or an OHT). Choose between these activities:
• **students listen and repeat selected words**
• **designated students read out words**

Exercise 1: Read and say

Exploit the visual. Demonstrate the vowel change from /ɒ/ to /əʊ/ when ~e is added. Explain that *rod*, *rode*, *red* and *read* (/riːd/) are for rapid review of vowel sounds separating *r* and *d*. Vary the procedure for the different sections. See Unit 25, Exercise 1 for suggestions.

Transcript 🔊 **3.12** (3 mins, 24 secs)

1 not **2** note **3** cod **4** code **5** hop **6** hope
7 rob **8** robe **9** pop **10** pope

1 hot **2** hotel **3** hoe **4** boat

1 bone **2** broke **3** code **4** cone **5** cope **6** cove
7 drove **8** home **9** hope **10** joke **11** lone
12 rode **13** rope **14** tone **15** vote **16** woke
17 probe **18** stone **19** stove **20** zone

1 motel **2** hotel **3** vote **4** note **5** bone **6** cone
7 lone **8** tone **9** stone **10** home **11** broke
12 joke **13** woke **14** cove **15** zone **16** hope
17 rope **18** drove **19** stove **20** probe

1 rod **2** rode **3** red **4** read **5** home **6** hot
7 broke **8** motel **9** wick **10** woke **11** wake
12 weak **13** zone **14** lone **15** loan **16** loon
17 noon **18** rope **19** probe **20** rob **21** robe
22 bone

Exercise 2: Listen and tick

Follow the usual procedure. Replay (or say again) any difficult pairs if students have difficulty.

Answers

not	woke	joke	mod	lobe	code	hop
home	stove	probe	rope	tone	zone	rode

Exercise 3: Fill in the spaces

Ask students to work out the missing word for each picture orally. Then ask them to write the answers in the spaces. Check to see that they can transliterate from print to basic handwriting.

Answers

From left to right: stone, brick, wood, rope, steel

Exercise 4: Read, then listen and check

The CD contains a sentence about the time in each location (It's ... in ...). Write on the board *It's six in Dallas*. Read it and ask students to repeat it. Now ask about Rome, China and Japan, and students reply using the *It's ... in ...* format. Now ask students to read the whole exercise silently. Allow a minute for this. Then play the CD.

The Texas West Hotel Dallas: time zones

It's six in Dallas.

It's one in Rome.

It's eight in China.

It's nine in Japan.

Exercise 5: Number the words, then listen and check

Show the students what to do by explaining the examples in the first line. Then allow three minutes for the students to complete this. Play the CD for students to check their answers.

1 *o* in *hot*	**2** *oo* in *zoo*	**3** *o* in *coat, no, foe, vote*
vote 3	hot 1	zoo 2
Rome 3	shoot 2	rope 3
roof 2	foam 3	so 3
coach 3	moon 2	sock 1
soon 2	stove 3	food 2
joke 3	toe 3	probe 3
go 3	hotel 3	goat 3

Exercise 6: Read, then listen and check

Tell students to read down the columns. Follow the normal procedure.

time zone	he woke up
a hotel in Rome	she drove home
a stone road	a safe zone
a hot stove	ride a bike
the green zone	he broke a bone

he is late home
don't park in this zone
don't stop in that zone
don't go home late
we won't be late

Exercise 7: Dictation

Follow the usual procedure.

Answers

1 home	**2** stone	**3** zone	**4** drove	**5** hotel

Closure

Put these words from the unit on the board (or OHT): *zone, bone, note, hope, joke* and *code*. Ask students to underline them in the Course Book. This is a reading exercise in itself. Ask students to learn the meaning of them before beginning the next unit.

Objectives
By the end of the lesson, students should be able to:

■ recognize and pronounce all the letters of the alphabet;

■ name selected letters of the alphabet.

Adaptations

Faster/mixed-ability classes	Directed self-study
In this unit, the objective is to be able to name and recognize the name of every letter in the alphabet and to introduce alphabetical order. Check students' ability to name the letters by selecting different letters for them to say aloud (use flashcards). If they have no difficulty here, begin with Exercise 3.	Explain that this unit is about the names of the 26 letters of the alphabet. Check students' ability to name the letters by selecting different ones for them to say aloud. On that basis, tell student(s) which exercises to do, recognizing they may need to practise writing capitals (Exercise 3). Remind them that they can replay the CD, or pause it, if they wish.

Words for revision
(also available as flashcards)

boat	bone	broke	cod	code	cone	cope
cove	drove	hoe	home	hop	hope	hot
hotel	joke	lone	motel	note	pop	pope
probe	rob	robe	rod	rode	rope	stone
stove	tone	vote	weak	wick	woke	zone

The letters of the alphabet for this lesson
(also available as flashcards)

A	B	C	D	E	F	G
H	I	J	K	L	M	N
O	P	Q	R	S	T	U
V	W	X	Y	Z		

Introduction
Write words from the revision list on the board/IWB (or use flashcards or an OHT). Choose between these activities:
• **students listen and repeat selected words**
• **designated students read out words**

Exercise 1: Read and say

This exercise teaches *z* as *zed*. It is recommended you teach *h* as *aitch* not *haitch*. This is the first time students learn the names of each letter, as opposed to the sound. It is important that students understand this. Exploit the visual. See who can read *ABC*. This gets across that this unit is about the names of letters, not the sounds they represent.

Read the first word in each of the rows 1–7. Ask the students to read the word at the beginning of each row. It is important that students get the vowel in each word right. Play the CD through to the end of row 7 (the end of section one). Play it again. Students repeat.

Then move on to the second section, where the whole alphabet is written out. Explain that the letters are in alphabetical order. Play this section on the CD. Students listen, while following in the Course Book. Play this section again. Students repeat each letter, while following in the Course Book. Play a game. Put each letter on a different card (or use the flashcards). Shuffle the cards. Students race to put them into alphabetical order.

Transcript ⊙ **3.18** (1 min, 57 secs)

1 see	B C D E G P T V
2 get	F L M N S X Z
3 day	A H J K
4 you	Q U W
5 hi	I Y
6 go	O
7 car	R

A B C D E F G H I J K L M N O P Q R S T U V W X Y Z

Exercise 2: Put the letters A–Z in the boxes with the same vowel sound

Students can work on this individually or with a partner. If working individually, students compare their answers with a partner when they have finished. Monitor and correct as they work. When they have finished, show the right answers on an OHT/IWB.

Answers

do	make	mean	men	so	park	pipe
Q U W	A H J K	B C D E G P T V	F L M N S X Z	O	R	I Y

Exercise 3: Trace and write

Follow the usual procedure. Monitor and correct.

Exercise 4: Dictation

This dictation differs from the previous dictation exercises. On the CD, the words are spelt out first (now that students have learnt the names of the letters), then the word is read. However, the usual procedure can be followed.

Answers

Transcript ● 3.19 (1 min, 57 secs)

1 H-O-M-E (home)	2 L-I-N-E (line)
3 M-A-Z-E (maze)	4 A-F-R-A-I-D (afraid)
5 S-T-O-N-E (stone)	6 C-H-I-N-A (China)
7 C-L-O-C-K (clock)	8 J-A-P-A-N (Japan)
9 B-R-I-D-E (bride)	10 Q-U-E-E-N (queen)

Exercise 5: Read, then listen and check

Vary the procedure for the different sections of this exercise. For the first section, let the students read the words silently. Then play the CD for that section only. Check pronunciation by giving the number of a word and asking individuals or the class to say it.

Set the second section as silent reading. Tell students to read down the columns. Then, to produce variation, test the words by asking students to volunteer what they think each word is. Write each selected word on the board. Do not spend too long on this phase. Then play the CD.

Lastly, the number plates. With a partner, students read them to each other. Monitor. Play the CD.

Transcript ● 3.20 (1 min, 42 secs)

1 wipe	2 time	3 Friday	4 Hi	5 I	6 hi-fi	7 pi
CD	DNA	OK	USA	BMW		www
http	UN	CNN	ABC	TDK		EU
CBS	MTV	L.A.	DVD-RW	VW		USB
iPod	eBay	a.m.	p.m.			

218 PXT   289 SKY   KZX 296   HWL 467

Exercise 6: Number from 1–6

Allow students to look at the six logos to familiarize themselves with them. Read the logos out in the order they appear on the page, to ensure they hear the same words from the CD. Play the CD, students number the logos in the order that they hear them. Check the answers with the students.

Answers

Transcript ● 3.21 (0 mins, 32 secs)

iPod   TDK   bbc.co.uk BBC home   USB   BMW CNN.com

Exercise 7: Read

Ask students to take this exercise a column at a time (from left to right). After they have read the first column silently, read it to them. Move on to the second column and ask the students to work out how to read it by reading silently. Refer them to Exercise 1 if they have any difficulties remembering individual letters. Ask for volunteers to read the third column. For the last column, ask students to read the website addresses to their partners. Monitor and correct. Read the addresses out as feedback.

Closure

Read out the letters of the alphabet in the right order. Do it again with students repeating each letter after you. Set students the task of learning to say the letters A–M in the right order before the next unit.

29   B L   C L   F L

Objectives

By the end of the lesson, students should be able to:

- associate sight and sound of the letters *bl, cl, fl, gl, pl* and *sl* as capitals and lower case in a variety of typefaces;

- demonstrate recognition and production of previously learnt letters, letter combinations and words.

Adaptations

Faster/mixed-ability classes	Directed self-study
Use Exercise 2 as a test. Also probe the students' ability to distinguish between *b* and *p* in *bl* and *pl* and between *c* and *g* in *cl* and *gl*. Go back to Exercise 1 only if necessary.	Go over the new letter combinations/sounds and probe the students' ability to distinguish between *b* and *p* in *bl* and *pl*, and between *c* and *g* in *cl* and *gl*. Tell student(s) which exercises to do. Remind them that they can replay the CD, or pause it, if they wish.

Letters for revision
(also available as flashcards)

A	B	C	D	E	F	G
H	I	J	K	L	M	N
O	P	Q	R	S	T	U
V	W	X	Y	Z		

New letters/words for this lesson
(also available as flashcards)

bl /bl/	cl /kl/	fl /fl/	gl /gl/	pl /pl/	sl /sl/
black	bleed	block	bloom	blush	clam	clap
clean	clock	club	flash	flat	flea	float
flock	glad	glen	glum	plan	plane	plate
play	plead	please	sleep	slot	slum	

Introduction

The closure task from Unit 28 was to learn the letters of the alphabet from A–M. Write these letters in a random order on the board/IWB (or use flashcards or an OHT). Then check who can recite the letters A–M, in the correct order. Then choose between these activities:

- **students listen and repeat selected letters**
- **individual designated students read out letters**

Exercise 1: Read and say

Exploit the visual. Follow the normal procedure.

Transcript 3.22 (3 mins, 22 secs)

1 bl **2** cl **3** fl **4** gl **5** pl **6** sl

1 b **2** br **3** bl **4** c **5** cr **6** cl **7** f **8** fr **9** fl
10 p **11** pr **12** pl **13** s **14** sl

1 back **2** black **3** cub **4** club **5** fat **6** flat
7 gum **8** glum **9** pan **10** plan **11** seep **12** sleep

1 bleed **2** block **3** bloom **4** blush **5** clap
6 clean **7** clock **8** flash **9** flea **10** float **11** glad
12 glen **13** gloom **14** plane **15** play **16** please
17 slap **18** slot **19** slope **20** slum

1 flea **2** sleep **3** clean **4** please **5** bleed
6 blush **7** club **8** clock **9** block **10** slot
11 gloom **12** bloom **13** float **14** slope **15** slap
16 clap **17** flat **18** glad **19** black **20** flash
21 plan **22** play **23** plane **24** glen **25** slum

Exercise 2: Listen and tick

Follow the usual procedure. Replay (or say again) any difficult pairs if students have difficulty.

Answers

Transcript 3.23 (0 mins, 45 secs)

back	black	cap	clap	clean	bleach	flash	frock
glad	plea	pay	pray	sleep	slot	sum	clam

Exercise 3: Trace and write

Monitor, to make sure students are writing the ascenders and descenders correctly. Follow the usual procedure.

Exercise 4: Read and label

Follow the usual procedure.

Answers

1 alarm clock   **2** float plane   **3** USB flash drive
4 black and green

Exercise 5: Find the different word

Follow the usual procedure.

Answers

play	*play*	(pray)	play	play
please	please	please	*please*	(plead)
clock	clock	(crock)	clock	clock
plane	(plate)	PLANE	*plane*	*plane*

Exercise 6: Find the words

The words in the two lists are on the remote control. Ask students to read the words aloud individually. Still working individually, students find where each word appears on the remote control. After one minute, solve any problems – students may have difficulty locating a word. Working with a partner, Student A reads a word and Student B points to it on the remote control. Then reverse roles.

Answers

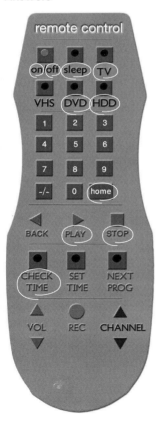

Exercise 7: Read, then listen and check

Follow the usual procedure.

Transcript 🔊 **3.24** (0 mins, 46 secs)

1 clock   **2** flock   **3** lot   **4** plot   **5** flat   **6** flash
7 boom   **8** bloom   **9** free   **10** flea   **11** pray
12 play   **13** pea   **14** plea   **15** please

Exercise 8: Read the key words

This exercise tests two things: the ability to read letters, and the ability to read key words already encountered that do not follow the rules, e.g. *don't*. Ask students to read through the list silently. Then, either using an OHT or by writing words from the list on the board/IWB, ask volunteers or nominated students to read out selected words from the list.

Transcript 🔊 **3.25** (0 mins, 21 secs)

OK   please   I   won't   you   and   do   don't   Hi
while

Exercise 9: Read, say and check

Tell students to read down the columns. Follow the usual procedure.

Transcript 🔊 **3.26** (0 mins, 47 secs)

yes, please	please wait
please stay	play an MP3
tea, please	USB flash drive
coffee, please	a black flash drive
glad to meet you	
go to sleep	
planes, boats and trains	
please clean this	

Closure

See if students recognize the logos at the foot of the page. With a partner, they can try to work out how to read them. Set students the task of learning to say the letters N–Z in the right order before the next unit.

30   ~ N D   ~ N K

Objectives
By the end of the lesson, students should be able to:

- associate sight and sound of the letters ~nd, ~nk, ~nt and ~nch as capitals and lower case in a variety of typefaces;
- demonstrate recognition and production of previously learnt letters, letter combinations and words.

Adaptations

Faster/mixed-ability classes	Directed self-study
Using an OHT/IWB, start with random words from Exercise 1 as a test. Focus on ~nch, the first three-letter cluster encountered. Begin with Exercise 3 if the performance on Exercise 1 allows.	Go over the new consonant clusters/sounds, paying particular attention to ~nch, the first three-letter cluster encountered. Tell student(s) which exercises to do. Remind them that they can replay the CD, or pause it, if they wish.

Words for revision
(also available as flashcards)

black	bleed	block	bloom	blush	clam	clap
clean	clock	club	flash	flat	flea	float
flock	glad	glen	glum	plan	plane	plate
play	plead	please	sleep	slot	slum	

New letters/words for this lesson
(also available as flashcards)

~nd /nd/   ~nk /ŋk/   ~nt /nt/   ~nch /ntʃ/

and	ant	band	bank	bench	bend	bond
brand	bunch	crunch	don't	drink	end	faint
fond	French	gland	grand	grunt	hand	Hank
hint	inch	ink	junk	land	lend	link
lunch	mint	pinch	pink	pond	print	punch
punk	quench	sent	tank	wench	went	wink

Introduction

First, check that students have completed the closure task from Unit 29 – learning the letters N–Z in alphabetical order. Then, write words from the revision list on the board/IWB (or use flashcards or an OHT). Choose between these activities:
- **students listen and repeat selected words**
- **designated students read out words**

Exercise 1: Read and say

Exploit the visual. This is a long exercise. Vary the procedure for each section; see the notes for Unit 25, Exercise 1 for suggestions.

Transcript 3.27 (4 mins, 8 secs)

1 nd   2 nk   3 nt   4 nch

1 and   2 ink   3 ant   4 inch

1 band   2 hand   3 land   4 blend   5 stand   6 gland
7 grand   8 end   9 fond   10 pond   11 bank
12 tank   13 drink   14 link   15 pink   16 junk
17 went   18 sent   19 don't   20 print   21 grunt
22 French   23 bunch   24 lunch   25 quench

1 land   2 lend   3 link   4 lunch   5 band   6 bend
7 bank   8 French   9 bunch   10 drink   11 drank
12 drunk   13 grunt   14 grand   15 end   16 gland
17 junk   18 quench   19 crunch   20 went   21 sent
22 pink   23 pinch   24 wink   25 bond

1 sink   2 paint   3 blond   4 bland   5 blend
6 trench   7 plank   8 prank   9 chunk   10 trunk
11 flinch   12 blink   13 crank   14 punk   15 punch
16 clink   17 brand   18 bench   19 faint   20 mint
21 hint   22 winch

Exercise 2: Listen and tick

Follow the usual procedure. Replay (or say again) any difficult pairs if students have difficulty.

Answers

Transcript 3.28 (0 mins, 41 secs)

ant   ink   hand   bank   drink   inch   pink

French   crush   bunch   went   link   end   bond

Exercise 3: Trace and write

Monitor, to make sure students are writing the ascenders correctly. Follow the usual procedure.

Exercise 4: Read and label

Follow the usual procedure.

Answers

1 ink   **2** bunch of grapes   **3** hand   **4** ant   **5** drink

Exercise 5: Find the different word

Follow the usual procedure.

Answers

end	*and*	end	end	END
lunch	lunch	*lunch*	bunch	LUNCH
DRINK	drunk	drink	*drink*	drink
went	went	want	went	*went*

Exercise 6: Find and circle words from Units 26–30

This is a new activity. Students can look back to each of the units to see which letters/letter combinations to look for in this exercise. Show the students what to do by completing a couple of examples on an OHT/IWB:

- Turn back to one of the units covered (not Unit 27, which is not represented in this exercise).
- Point out which sound(s) the unit covered.
- Going back to Exercise 6, find a word with the sounds from the unit just looked at and circle it.

Don't mention that Unit 27 is not represented. Ask the students to continue, beginning with words from this unit (30).

Answers

Unit 26 I~E: (web)site, time, line (x2)
Unit 28 A B C D E: A a, p.m.,
Unit 29 BL CL FL GL PL SL: clip, black, blue
Unit 30 ~ND ~NK ~NT ~NCH: print, paint, font, pink

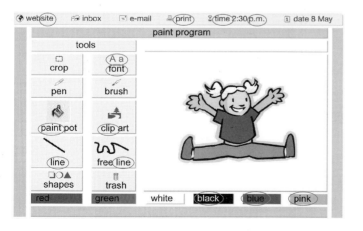

Exercise 7: Read, then listen and check.

Tell the students to read down the columns. Follow the usual procedure.

a grandstand	a weblink	eat and drink	punch drunk
Land's End	a pink drink	eat lunch	a punk band
stop junk mail	a black tank	end lunch	a mint drink
send junk mail	a French bank	lunchtime	a French man

Exercise 8: Dictation

Follow the usual procedure.

Answers

1 bank card   **2** black ink   **3** big bunch   **4** hot lunch
5 brand name   **6** went home

Closure

Ask students to learn the meaning of the words from Units 26–30 that appear in the picture in Exercise 6.

Objectives

By the end of the lesson, students should be able to:

- associate the sight and sound of the letter combinations *sc*, *sk*, *sm*, *sn*, *sp* and *sw* as capitals and lower case in a variety of typefaces;

- demonstrate recognition and production of previously learnt letters, letter combinations and words.

Adaptations

Faster/mixed-ability classes	Directed self-study
Start with Exercise 4 as a test. Ask students to say the words *switch*, etc. Start with this exercise if they can read the words and go back to the earlier exercises only if necessary.	Check the new consonant clusters/sounds by practising the first section of Exercise 1. Tell student(s) which exercises to do. Remind them that they can replay the CD, or pause it, if they wish.

Words for revision
(also available as flashcards)

and	ant	band	bank	bench	bend	bond
brand	bunch	crunch	don't	drink	end	faint
fond	French	gland	grand	grunt	hand	Hank
hint	inch	ink	junk	land	lend	link
lunch	mint	pinch	pink	pond	print	punch
punk	quench	sent	tank	wench	went	wink

New letters/words for this lesson
(also available as flashcards)

sc /sk/	sk /sk/	sm /sm/	sn /sn/	sp /sp/	sw /sw/
escape	scan	scar	scart	scat	skid	skin
skip	skunk	smack	smart	smash	smile	smock
smug	snack	snail	snake	snap	snarl	snatch
sneak	sniff	snip	snub	Spain	spam	spark
speak	speed	spend	spike	spin	spine	spit
spite	spook	spoon	spot	spun	swam	sweep
sweet	swim	swipe	Swiss	switch	swoon	

Introduction

Write words from the revision list on the board/IWB (or use flashcards or an OHT). Choose between these activities:
- **students listen and repeat selected words**
- **designated students read out words**

Exercise 1: Read and say

Exploit the visual. Follow the normal procedure.

Transcript 🔊 3.31 (4 mins, 16 secs)

1 s **2** sk **3** sc **4** sm **5** sn **6** sp **7** sw

1 scan **2** skin **3** smug **4** snap **5** spot **6** swim

1 skip **2** scar **3** SCART **4** escape **5** spam
6 speak **7** speed **8** spoon **9** spend **10** Spain
11 smack **12** smash **13** smart **14** smile **15** snip
16 snack **17** snake **18** snail **19** sneak **20** swam
21 sweep **22** sweet **23** swipe **24** switch

1 spam **2** swam **3** snap **4** snack **5** smack
6 snail **7** escape **8** snake **9** Spain **10** skin
11 switch **12** swipe **13** smile **14** swim **15** smug
16 speak **17** sweet **18** speed **19** sweep
20 spoon **21** smart **22** SCART **23** spend **24** spot
25 spook

1 skid **2** scoot **3** swoop **4** smock **5** snub
6 spun **7** Swiss **8** sniff **9** snarl **10** snatch
11 spook **12** spark **13** spine **14** spite **15** spit
16 spike **17** scoop **18** snug **19** swoon **20** skunk
21 swain **22** scat

Exercise 2: Number from 1–7

Follow the usual procedure.

Answers

Transcript 🔊 3.32 (0 mins, 29 secs)

1 spin **2** smart **3** skin **4** sweet **5** scar **6** sin
7 snake

Exercise 3: Listen and tick

Follow the usual procedure.

Answers

spam	escape	skin	mug	spot	sweet	nail
spend	smack	speak	sake	when	seat	spoon

Exercise 4: Read and label

Follow the usual procedure.

Answers

1 speak　**2** smile　**3** snake　**4** switch　**5** Spain

Exercise 5: Find the different word

Follow the usual procedure.

Answers

switch	switch	switch	(snitch)
speak	(speed)	speak	**speak**
smile	smile	(snail)	*smile*
(skin)	swim	*swim*	swim

Exercise 6: Find and circle words from Units 26–31

The words the students need to find contain the spellings covered in Units 26–31. There aren't any words from Units 27 and 29, but don't tell students this.

Answers
Unit 26 I~E: time
Unit 28 A B C D E: DVDs, DVD
Unit 30 ~ND ~NK ~NT ~NCH: print, rent, spend (x3)
Unit 31 SC SK SM SN SP SW: escape, Spain, snakes (x2), snail, speak, smile, sweet, speed, smash, spooks, swim, switch (x2), SMART, SCART, Swiss

Exercise 7: Read, then listen and check

Follow the usual procedure.

a hotel swipe card	a TV SCART
swim, swam, swum	snakes on a plane
a Swiss SMART car	a smart swipe card

spam and junk mail
stop spam e-mail
send spam

Exercise 8: Dictation

Follow the usual procedure.

Answers

1 escape	E-S-C-A-P-E	escape
2 switch	S-W-I-T-C-H	switch
3 smash	S-M-A-S-H	smash
4 spoke	S-P-O-K-E	spoke
5 snarl	S-N-A-R-L	snarl

Closure

Ask students to learn the meaning of the words from Units 26–31 that appear in the picture in Exercise 6.

Objectives

By the end of the lesson, students should be able to:

- associate the sight and sound of the letters ~*ng* in words of one or two syllables, in a variety of typefaces;

- write a place name, beginning the name with a capital letter;

- recognize and pronounce the nationalities referred to;

- write a nationality, beginning the word with a capital letter;

- demonstrate an awareness of key irregular spellings: *Eng* for /ɪŋ/ in *English*, and *j* for /ʤ/ in *Bejing*.

- demonstrate recognition and production of previously learnt letters, letter combinations and words

Adaptations

Faster/mixed-ability classes	Directed self-study
As in previous units, you could start with Exercise 4 as a reading test, and go back to the earlier exercises only if necessary. In using Exercise 4 as a test, make sure students are actually pronouncing *ng* correctly.	Go over the new consonant cluster and its sound. Make sure students are actually pronouncing *ng* as /ŋ/. Tell student(s) which exercises to do. Remind students they can replay the CD, or pause it, if they wish.

Notes on new sounds

The velar nasal /ŋ/ is difficult for some speakers. Where this is the case for your students, exemplify and practise the difference between /ŋ/ and its spelling ~*ng* from the alveolar nasal /n/ and its spelling ~*n*.

Words for revision
(also available as flashcards)

escape	scan	scar	scart	skid	skin
skip	skunk	smack	smart	smash	smile
smock	smug	snack	snail	snake	snap
snarl	snatch	sneak	sniff	snip	snub
Spain	spam	spark	speak	speed	spend
spike	spin	spine	spit	spite	spook
spoon	spot	spun	swam	sweep	sweet
swim	swipe	Swiss	switch	swoon	

New letters/words for this lesson
(also available as flashcards)

~ng /ŋ/

ban	bang	banging	Bangkok	Bangladesh
Beijing	bring	bringing	British	cling
doing	drinking	Dutch	eating	English
fling	French	going	Greek	hang
Hong Kong	king	long	playing	rang
reading	ring	ringing	rung	sang
saying	Shanghai	sing	singing	slang
sling	song	speaking	sting	stung
swing	Swiss	swung	wing	

Introduction

Write selected words from the revision list on the board/IWB (or use flashcards or an OHT). Choose between these activities:

- **students listen and repeat selected words**
- **designated students read out words**

Exercise 1: Read and say

Exploit the visual – an illustration of *King Kong*. Follow the normal procedure.

Optionally, you could do Exercise 3 when you have finished the third section of Exercise 1, and resume section four after doing Exercise 3. Note that *lon* is a nonsense word.

Transcript 🔊 **3.36** (2 mins, 36 secs)

1 ing **2** ang **3** ong **4** ung

1 win **2** wing **3** ban **4** bang **5** lon **6** long
7 run **8** rung

1 king **2** ring **3** sing **4** wing **5** bring **6** cling
7 fling **8** sling **9** sting **10** swing **11** bang
12 hang **13** rang **14** sang **15** slang **16** long
17 song **18** rung **19** stung **20** swung

1 sing **2** singing **3** ring **4** ringing **5** bring
6 bringing **7** bang **8** banging **9** drink **10** drinking
11 eat **12** eating **13** go **14** going **15** do
16 doing **17** speak **18** speaking **19** read
20 reading **21** play **22** playing **23** say **24** saying

Exercise 2: Listen and tick

Follow the usual procedure.

Answers

Transcript 🔊 **3.37** (0 mins, 41 secs)

ban sing ran king stun hand cling

ring bringing paying meeting reading
swinging banging

Exercise 3: Trace and write

Follow the usual procedure.

Exercise 4: Complete the sentences

Ensure that the students understand what it is they are
completing – easy sentences in the present progressive.
The verbs are high frequency. However, if students have
problems with meaning, preview the meanings of the verbs.
Before the class completes the exercise individually, do the
first one (*He is + drinking*) on the board/IWB (or use an OHT)
with the class.

Answers

1 drinking **2** eating **3** reading **4** sleeping **5** singing

Exercise 5: Circle the CAPITAL letters

Demonstrate capital and lower-case letters on the board as a
reminder. Then tell the students how to do the exercise. Give
or elicit the answers. Revise the names of each capital letter
used in the exercise.

Answers

Ⓔnglish Ⓑeijing Ⓒhina Ⓑangkok Ⓑritish ⒽongⓀong
Ⓑangladesh

Exercise 6: Label the flags

Explain *flag* using an OHT/IWB – students count the flags.
Elicit the number of flags. Ask students to work with a
partner to decide which flag is which. Allow one minute
for this. Ask students for their answers.

Answers

1 English **2** French **3** Swiss **4** Dutch **5** British

Exercise 7: Read, then listen and check

Draw students' attention to the correct pronunciation and
spelling of *English* and *Beijing*. Get the students to repeat the
pronunciation of **English** and *Beijing*. Ask the students to look
at the words with capital letters. They are all place names or
nationalities. Then follow the usual procedure. At the end,
revise the names of each capital letter used in the exercise.

Transcript 🔊 **3.38** (0 mins, 59 secs)

1 English **2** Beijing **3** Shanghai **4** Hong Kong
5 Bangladesh **6** Bangkok **7** British

1 A British plane **2** A Swiss bank **3** A Greek flag
4 A Dutch car **5** An English man **6** A French boat

Exercise 8: Dictation

Follow the usual procedure.

Answers

Transcript 🔊 **3.39** (1 min, 15 secs)

1 Capital H o-n-g Capital K o-n-g Hong Kong

2 Capital B a-n-g-l–a-d-e-s-h Bangladesh

3 Capital S h-a-n-g-h-a-i Shanghai

4 Capital B e-i-j-i-n-g Beijing

Closure

Ask students to find and read out the place names on the
four pictures after the dictation.

Objectives

By the end of the lesson, students should be able to:

- associate the sight of the letters *or, ore* and *aw* with the one vowel sound /ɔː/ in capitals and lower case, in words of one or two syllables;

- read and spell *four(teen), your* and *door/poor,* etc., as spellings of the same vowel sound /ɔː/;

- demonstrate recognition and production of previously learnt letters and letter combinations and words.

Adaptations

Faster/mixed-ability classes	Directed self-study
Use Exercise 5 as a reading test to see if students can recognize each letter sequence as representing the same sound (/ɔː/). If they can, begin there. Go back to the earlier exercises only if necessary.	Go over the new letter combinations and their sound (/ɔː/). Check students recognize each letter sequence as representing the same sound (/ɔː/). Tell student(s) which exercises to do. Remind them that they can replay the CD, or pause it, if they wish.

Notes on new sounds

Although the new sound here can be represented by letter combinations including consonants, *or(e)* and *aw*, it is important for students to fully understand that the target sound /ɔː/ is a pure vowel and neither consonant is sounded in British English Received Pronunciation (RP).

Words for revision
(also available as flashcards)

ban	bang	banging	Bangkok	Bangladesh
Beijing	bring	bringing	British	cling
doing	drinking	Dutch	eating	English
fling	French	going	Greek	hang
Hong Kong	king	lon	long	playing
rang	reading	ring	ringing	rung
sang	saying	Shanghai	sing	singing
slang	sling	song	speaking	sting
stung	swing	Swiss	swung	wing

New letters/words for this lesson
(also available as flashcards)

or /ɔː/   ore /ɔː/   aw /ɔː/

born	chore	core	dawn	door	draw
drawn	floor	for	fork	four	fourteen
jaw	law	lawn	moor	more	morning
or	poor	prawn	saw	score	short
sort	sport	store	storm	swore	torch
your					

Introduction

Write selected words from the revision list on the board/IWB (or use flashcards or an OHT). Choose between these activities:

- **students listen and repeat selected words**
- **designated students read out words**

Exercise 1: Read and say

Exploit the visual – the Ford logo. Draw students' attention to the words *your* and *four* that follow the plus (+) sign in the second section. They are important words containing the target vowel of the unit which are spelt in an exceptional way. Otherwise, follow the normal procedure.

> ### Transcript ⏺ 3.40 (2 mins, 35 secs)
>
> **1** o   **2** oo   **3** oa   **4** or   **5** ore   **6** oor   **7** aw
>
> **1** or   **2** for   **3** more   **4** door   **5** saw   **6** your   **7** four
>
> **1** born   **2** fork   **3** morning   **4** short   **5** sort
> **6** sport   **7** storm   **8** torch   **9** core   **10** chore
> **11** score   **12** store   **13** swore   **14** poor   **15** moor
> **16** floor   **17** four   **18** your   **19** law   **20** jaw
> **21** saw   **22** draw   **23** dawn   **24** prawn   **25** lawn
>
> **1** more   **2** moor   **3** morning   **4** saw   **5** swore
> **6** storm   **7** law   **8** lawn   **9** born   **10** drawn
> **11** prawn   **12** jaw   **13** your   **14** for   **15** four
> **16** floor   **17** torch   **18** chore   **19** Ford

Exercise 2: Number from 1–7

Follow the usual procedure.

Answers

1 four   **2** your   **3** score   **4** chore   **5** jaw   **6** store
7 fork

1 sort   **2** short   **3** poor   **4** spot   **5** born   **6** shot
7 sport

Exercise 3: Listen and tick

Follow the usual procedure.

Answers

sort   pot   lawn   four   jaw   spot   for

short   shot   prawn   chore   draw   store   or

Exercise 4: Trace and write

Follow the usual procedure.

Exercise 5: Read and label

Follow the usual procedure.

Answers

1 door   **2** four   **3** fork   **4** torch   **5** score

Exercise 6: Match the same words

This provides practice in reading different fonts, handwriting, capitals and lower case. Students read the first column and find the same words in the second column. Students do the same for the second table. Although not essential, they could join up the two examples of each word with a line. It is a good idea to set them a time limit according to their ability, to produce a little pressure but no panic.

Exercise 7: Find words from Unit 33

This exercise is best used as the Closure. Students complete this individually. Set a reasonable time limit. Students compare answers with a partner. Give feedback and assessment: *How many words did you find? What are they?*

Answers

N	F	L	O	O	R	J	H
M	O	R	N	I	N	G	X
B	U	J	Q	M	O	R	E
D	R	A	W	L	R	S	Y
Z	P	W	X	A	T	A	O
B	O	R	N	W	H	W	U
M	O	S	C	O	R	E	R
P	R	A	W	N	P	A	W

Exercise 8: Read, then listen and check

Follow the usual procedure.

4   14   15   16   17   19
four   fourteen   fifteen   sixteen   seventeen   nineteen

a car / a Ford car / four doors / a four-door car
a four-door Ford car / your car / your four-door car
a sports car / a four-door sports car / born
born at dawn / born in the morning /
I was born in May / sweetcorn / eat sweetcorn
prawns / sweetcorn and prawns / a storm /
rain and storm / law / court / a law court /
in a law court

Exercise 9: Dictation

Follow the usual procedure.

Answers

1 It is a four-door Ford   f-o-u-r d-o-o-r capital F o-r-d

2 He was born in the morning

Closure

Use Exercise 7 (see above).

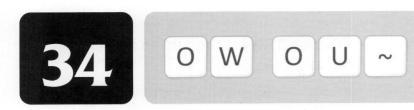
Objectives

By the end of the lesson, students should be able to:

- associate and read the letters *ow* and *ou* with the diphthong /aʊ/ in capitals and lower case, in words of one, two and three syllables and in a variety of typefaces;

- contrast the new letter combinations with *or* /ɔː/, *ore* /ɔː/ and *aw* /ɔː/ previously learnt;

- start initial exclamations with a capital letter;

- demonstrate recognition and production of previously learnt letters, letter combinations and words.

Adaptations

Faster/mixed-ability classes	Directed self-study
Start with Exercise 5 as a reading test, and go back to Exercise 1 only if necessary. Otherwise, start at Exercise 4.	Go over the new letter combinations and their sound (/aʊ/). Make sure that *w* is not sounded in any way. Tell student(s) which exercises to do. Remind them that they can replay the CD, or pause it, if they wish.

Notes on new sounds

The diphthong /aʊ/ is another vowel that can be represented by a letter combination containing a consonant which is not sounded in any way (*w*). It is important for students to fully understand that the target sound /aʊ/ is a pure vowel – the consonant is not sounded in British English Received Pronunciation (RP).

Words for revision
(also available as flashcards)

born	chore	core	dawn	door	draw
drawn	floor	for	fork	four	fourteen
jaw	law	lawn	moor	more	morning
or	poor	prawn	saw	score	short
sort	sport	store	storm	swore	torch
your					

New letters/words for this lesson
(also available as flashcards)

ow /aʊ/   ou~ /aʊ/

about	brown	cloud	clown	count	cow
crowd	crown	down	drown	found	fountain
gown	ground	hound	how	loud	morning
mount	mountain	noun	now	out	Ow!
pound	proud	prow	round	shout	snout
sound	town	vow	Wow!		

Introduction

Write selected words from the revision list on the board/IWB (or use flashcards or an OHT). Choose between these activities:

- **students listen and repeat selected words**
- **designated students read out words**

Exercise 1: Read and say

Exploit the visual – the *out* sign. Follow the normal procedure. Point out that *ow* can occur within a word and at the end of a word, while *ou* can only occur within a word, never at the end.

Transcript 🔊 3.45 (3 mins, 23 secs)

1 o   2 or   3 ore   4 ow   5 ou

1 now   2 how   3 out   4 about   5 loud   6 sound

1 how   2 now   3 cow   4 vow   5 Wow!   6 down
7 gown   8 town   9 brown   10 clown   11 crowd
12 crown   13 drown   14 out   15 shout   16 loud
17 cloud   18 proud   19 found   20 round   21 sound
22 ground   23 count   24 pound   25 about

1 out   2 now   3 drown   4 count   5 ground
6 town   7 cloud   8 brown   9 vow   10 shout
11 cow   12 drown   13 pound   14 gown   15 sound
16 down   17 round   18 crown   19 crowd   20 loud
21 cloud   22 found   23 Wow!   24 about   25 how

1 mount   2 hound   3 noun   4 snout   5 shouting
6 counting   7 drowning   8 prow   9 crowding
10 rounding

Exercise 2: Number from 1–7

Follow the usual procedure.

Answers

1 out **2** nor **3** proud **4** now **5** down **6** no
7 round

Exercise 3: Listen and tick

Follow the usual procedure.

Answers

Ow! town drown clown crowd pound vow
ground now loud out cow sound proud

Exercise 4: Trace and write

Follow the usual procedure.

Exercise 5: Read and label

Follow the usual procedure.

Answers

1 cloud **2** brown cow **3** crowd **4** pound **5** down

Exercise 6: Find the different word

Follow the normal procedure.

Answers

now	now	(noun)	now	now
how?	how?	How?	(now?)	how?
about	about	(around)	about	about
out	(our)	out	out	out

Exercise 7: Read, say and check

The first phase should be silent while the students apply knowledge and test their understanding. Working word by word through the list, invite volunteers to read out each word; accept good answers and gently reject ones you can't accept, inviting another try from someone else. In the event of time being short, there is no need to do all the phrases, just a credible sample. The listening phase is intended to be the last of the exercise, but students could repeat the words to reinforce the learning, particularly where syllable stress may be an issue (e.g., ho'tel, seven'teen).

a•bout	about
round•a•bout	roundabout
mount•ain	mountain
fount•ain	fountain
down•town	downtown
morn•ing	morning
es•cape	escape
Eng•lish	English
four•teen	fourteen
sev•en•teen	seventeen
ho•tel	hotel
rail•way	railway
pro•gram	program

Exercise 8: Read, then listen and check

Students read the phrases silently (1–2 minutes). Then follow the usual procedure.

a downtown car park   a mountain railway
a dark brown cow   down a mountain
about ten o'clock   a book about the town
shout out loud   go round and round
a loud sound   fourteen pounds

a town fountain
a big roundabout
look around the town
a ground-floor flat
I found a pound

Closure

Ask students to learn the meaning of the following words before the next lesson: *cloud, crowd, ground-floor flat, loud* and *shout*.

Objectives

By the end of the lesson, students should be able to:

■ associate and read ~y in capitals and lower case in a variety of typefaces, in words of one, two and three syllables, in the following contexts:

- as a final letter following a consonant or *u* in one-syllable words (/aɪ/ as in *by* or *buy*)

- as a final letter following a consonant in words of two or more syllables (/iː/ as in *daddy*)

- after a single *a* (/eɪ/ as in *play*)

- between two consonants, the second followed by *e* (/aɪ/ as in *byte*)

■ read the first vowel and the double consonant in words like *daddy* and *lobby*;

■ demonstrate recognition and production of previously learnt letters, letter combinations and words.

Adaptations

Faster/mixed-ability classes	Directed self-study
The point here is the difference between the pronunciation of *y* in *my* and *happy*, for example. Start with Exercise 3 as a reading test, and go back to the earlier exercises only if necessary. Otherwise, complete Exercise 3 and work through the unit from there.	The point here is the difference between the pronunciation of *y* in *my* and *happy*, for example. Go over the letter in the chosen contexts (see the Objectives). Explain to students that a double consonant is one sound NOT two (e.g., *happy*, *lobby*, etc.). Tell student(s) which exercises to do. Remind them that they can replay the CD, or pause it, if they wish.

Words for revision
(also available as flashcards)

about	brown	cloud	clown	count	cow
crowd	crown	down	drown	found	fountain
gown	ground	hound	how	loud	morning
mount	mountain	noun	now	out	Ow!
pound	proud	prow	round	shout	snout
sound	town	vow	Wow!		

New letters/words for this lesson
(also available as flashcards)

~y /eɪ/	~y /aɪ/	~y /iː/	~y /i/		
angry	buy	by	byte	choppy	cloudy
cry	daddy	Danny	dry	fly	funny
Getty	grubby	guy	happy	hi-fi	hippy
hungry	jetty	lobby	lorry	may	megabyte
mummy	my	nanny	ply	pry	rainy
say	shy	silly	sky	slay	sly
spy	sunny	try	why	Wi-Fi	windy

Introduction

Write selected words from the revision list on the board/IWB (or use flashcards or an OHT). Choose between these activities:

- **students listen and repeat selected words**
- **designated students read out words**

Exercise 1: Read and say

None of the sounds in this unit is new. What is new is their occurrence determined by the context in which *y* occurs. It is essential to explain to students that a double consonant is one sound, NOT two (e.g., *happy*, *lobby*, etc.). Exploit the visual. Draw students' attention to the words *buy* and *guy* that follow the plus (+) sign in section one. They are two important words containing the target vowel of the unit, but are spelt in an exceptional way. Then follow the normal procedure. As it is a long exercise, vary the presentation. For ideas, look back at the notes for Exercise 1 in Unit 25.

1 I 2 Hi 3 by 4 my 5 why 6 buy 7 guy

1 E 2 fun 3 funny 4 dad 5 daddy 6 wind
7 windy

1 by 2 cry 3 dry 4 fly 5 fry 6 ply 7 pry
8 my 9 sky 10 sly 11 spy 12 try 13 why
14 buy 15 guy 16 byte 17 megabyte 18 Wi-Fi
19 hi-fi

1 happy 2 lobby 3 lorry 4 jetty 5 funny
6 mummy 7 daddy 8 nanny 9 choppy
10 grubby 11 sunny 12 windy 13 cloudy
14 rainy 15 silly 16 angry 17 hungry

1 happy 2 daddy 3 windy 4 silly 5 rainy
6 cloudy 7 choppy 8 sunny 9 my 10 try 11 fry
12 cry 13 byte 14 sky 15 fly 16 sly 17 guy
18 dry 19 by 20 why 21 guy 22 angry
23 hungry 24 buy

1 dying 2 drying 3 crying 4 flying 5 frying
6 lying 7 spying 8 trying 9 buying

Exercise 2: Listen and tick

Follow the usual procedure.

Answers

my   sky   byte   fry   ply   try   Hi

lorry   happy   funny   hungry   jetty   daddy   Wi-Fi

Exercise 3: Trace and write

Follow the usual procedure. Make sure the students write *y* with a descender.

Exercise 4: Tick (✓) the same sounds and cross (✗) the different sounds

Using the example to explain, emphasize it is the vowel sound (not the consonants) that the students must judge as the same or different in each pair. Students should do this individually. Allow two minutes. Monitor. Then students can check each other's work with a partner. Feed back the answers with an OHT/IWB with word pairs ticked or crossed.

Answers

1 ✓ 2 ✓ 3 ✗ 4 ✗ 5 ✓ 6 ✗ 7 ✗ 8 ✓

Exercise 5: Listen to the weather reports for Shanghai and Tokyo and tick the words you hear

Set the exercise by talking about the weather outside. Explain that students do not need to understand every word. This exercise will need careful setting because this is the first time students have done a semi-authentic listening task. Play the CD. Play it again if necessary. Give the answers.

Answers

... and in Shanghai it will be **dry** and **sunny** in the morning. It will **rain** about two o'clock, and it will be **wet** and **cloudy**.

Tokyo will be **hot**, but **wet** on Sunday. It will be **windy**, with bad **storms** and lots of **rain**.

Exercise 6: Add the key words, then listen and check

This exercise reinforces alphabetical order, which was covered in Unit 28 and the Closures for Units 28 and 29. Ask students to recall the letters of the alphabet in the right order. Put each letter on the board/IWB or OHT as it is recalled. Say them all in order. Then remove them from view. Ask the class to look at the key words and the words each side of the gaps to see if they get the point. Use the first word as an example. Students do the rest individually. Set a suitable time limit. Play the CD.

Answers

a about am an and & at @ be **been** bit born but by can count day did do doing don't **down** drink each eat English for from get go going got had he Hi **him** how if I in it just let lot may me **mean** morning much must my no not now OK on **or** out please pound read room saw **say** see seen she shop so soon than that **the** them this too up us we went when which while **why** with won't yes you your

Exercise 7: Find and circle words from Unit 35

Ask the students to circle the words from the unit. Ask them to read them out.

Answers

Closure

Use Exercise 7 as the Closure as it consolidates the learning of the unit.

85

36  O Y ~ O I ~

Objectives

By the end of the lesson, students should be able to:

■ associate and read *oy* and *~oi~* in capitals and lower case in a variety of typefaces as /ɔɪ/;

■ demonstrate recognition and production of previously learnt letters, letter combinations and words.

Adaptations

Faster/mixed-ability classes	Directed self-study
As in previous units, you could start with Exercise 4 as a test, and go back to the earlier exercises only if necessary. Otherwise, begin by completing Exercise 4 and then work through the rest of the unit.	Go over the new combinations by running through section two of Exercise 1. On the basis of performance here, tell student(s) which exercises to do. Remind them that they can replay the CD, or pause it, if they wish.

Words for revision

(also available as flashcards)

angry	buy	by	byte	choppy	cloudy
cry	daddy	Danny	dry	fly	funny
Getty	grubby	guy	happy	hi-fi	hippy
hungry	jetty	lobby	lorry	may	megabyte
mummy	my	nanny	ply	pry	rainy
say	shy	silly	sky	slay	sly
spy	sunny	try	why	Wi-Fi	windy

New letters/words for this lesson

(also available as flashcards)

oy /ɔɪ/   ~oi~ /ɔɪ/

annoy	annoying	avoid	avoiding	boil	boiling	boy
coil	coin	coy	employ	enjoy	enjoying	foil
join	joining	joint	joy	loin	loyal	oil
point	pointing	royal	soil	soy	soya	spoil
toil	toy					

Introduction

Write words from the revision list on the board/IWB (or use flashcards or an OHT). Choose between these activities:
• **students listen and repeat selected words**
• **designated students read out words**

Exercise 1: Read and say

The key sounds in this unit are not new. What is new is the spelling distinction between *oi* within a word, and *oy* at the end (or before *~ing*, etc.), for the sound /ɔɪ/. Exploit the visual. Follow the normal procedure. The 'dark l' sound in words like *oil* and *boil* should not be overarticulated (too retroflex). As it is a long exercise, vary the presentation. For ideas, look back at the notes for Exercise 1 in Unit 25.

Exercise 2: Number from 1–7

Follow the usual procedure.

Answers

Exercise 3: Listen and tick

Follow the usual procedure.

Answers

toy	spoil	boy	join	joint	soy	coin
appoint	avoid	enjoy	oil	royal	join	soya

Exercise 4: Trace and write

Follow the usual procedure. Make sure the students write *y* with a descender.

Exercise 5: Number the words, then listen and check

Show the students what to do by explaining the example. Allow three minutes for this. Play the CD for students to check their answers.

Answers

1 = *o* in *hot*　**2** = *oi/oy* in *boy*
3 = *o* in *coat, foe, vote*　**4** = *or* in *born*

soap 3	lot 1	toy 2	born 4
drawn 4	point 2	don't 3	woke 3
hotel 3	cord 4	job 1	spoil 2
rope 3	boil 2	joy 2	fond 1
boy 2	song 1	bone 3	more 4
joint 2	poor 4	torch 4	hope 3
swore 4	soil 2	stove 3	prawn 4
annoy 2	snob 1	floor 4	spot 1
long 1	got 1	avoid 2	coin 2

Exercise 6: Read, then listen and check

Follow the usual procedure.

a pound coin	boil sweetcorn
a round coin	point at the floor
four-megabyte	bones and joints
soya bean	boiling oil
coins and cards	
a boy and a toy	
soil and toil	
enjoy your lunch	

Exercise 7: Dictation

Follow the usual procedure.

Answers

1 enjoy　**2** point　**3** loyal　**4** oil　**5** avoid

Exercise 8: Find words with *oi / oy*

Ask the students to circle the words containing *oi* or *oy*. Ask them to read them out.

Answers

Closure

Learn the meanings of the words in the dictation for next lesson.

37   I R   U R   O R

Objectives

By the end of the lesson, students should be able to:

- associate and read *ir, ur* and *or* as the pure vowel /ɜː/ in capitals and lower case in a variety of typefaces, in words of one or two syllables;

- distinguish the vowel in *wor + consonant* (/ɜː/) from other occurrences of *or* (/ɔː/);

- recognize and read *er* as /ɜː/ in *her* and *herb*;

- demonstrate recognition and production of previously learnt letters, letter combinations and words.

Adaptations

Faster/mixed-ability classes	Directed self-study
As in previous units, you could start with Exercise 4 as a test. Start at the beginning of Exercise 1 if the results of the test warrant it.	Go over the new letter combinations in all the different contexts covered in this unit (see the Objectives). On the basis of their performance, tell student(s) which exercises to do. Remind them that they can replay the CD, or pause it, if they wish.

Notes on new sounds

The new vowel /ɜː/ is spelt in various ways which are covered in this unit. *Wor* /wɜː/ rhymes with *her* when followed by one or more consonants.

Words for revision
(also available as flashcards)

annoy	annoying	avoid	avoiding	boil	boiling
boy	coil	coin	coy	employ	enjoy
enjoying	foil	join	joining	joint	joy
loin	loyal	oil	point	pointing	royal
soil	soy	soya	spoil	toil	toy

New letters/words for this lesson
(also available as flashcards)

ir /ɜː/   ur /ɜː/   or /ɜː/

bird	blur	burn	burning	burst	church
curl	first	flirt	fur	girl	Hamburg
her	herb	lurk	shirt	sir	skirt
spur	stir	surf	surfing	swirl	tore
turban	turf	Turk	turn	turning	whirl
word	wore	work	working	world	worm
worst					

Introduction

Write words from the revision list on the board/IWB (or use flashcards or an OHT). Choose between these activities:

- **students listen and repeat selected words**
- **designated students read out words**

Exercise 1: Read and say

Exploit the visual. Explain that the unit focuses on one vowel (/ɜː/) being spelt in four different ways. Draw students' attention to the word *her* that follows the plus (+) sign in the first section. It is an important word containing the target vowel of the unit, but is spelt in an exceptional way. Then follow the normal procedure.

Transcript ● 4.11 (2 mins, 44 secs)

1 ar   **2** or   **3** oy   **4** ir   **5** ur   **6** her   **7** word

1 sir   **2** bird   **3** first   **4** fur   **5** surf   **6** her   **7** world

1 bird   **2** first   **3** girl   **4** sir   **5** fur   **6** flirt   **7** skirt
8 shirt   **9** stir   **10** swirl   **11** her   **12** burn
13 church   **14** curl   **15** burst   **16** blur   **17** lurk
18 surf   **19** spur   **20** turn   **21** Turk   **22** word
23 work   **24** worst   **25** worm   **26** world   **27** herb

1 fur   **2** first   **3** turn   **4** surf   **5** spur   **6** burn
7 blur   **8** burst   **9** worst   **10** bird   **11** word   **12** her
13 girl   **14** curl   **15** Turk   **16** lurk   **17** work   **18** flirt
19 shirt   **20** sir   **22** skirt   **23** herb   **24** church
25 swirl

Exercise 2: Number from 1–7

Follow the normal procedure.

Answers

1 girl	**2** her	**3** work	**4** turn	**5** word	**6** first
7 sir					

Exercise 3: Listen and tick

Follow the usual procedure.

Answers

shirt	work	burn	first	sir	Turk	spur
fist	bird	for	shot	word	warm	curl

Exercise 4: Trace and write

Follow the usual procedure. Check the ascenders and descenders.

Exercise 5: Complete the sentences

This exercise depends on world knowledge and on understanding the meaning of the words and sentences as a whole, not on how the words are pronounced. In particular, teach *surf the net*. Ask the students what kind of word can follow *He is* ... from the list. This will help guide the students to the meanings of the words.

Answers

1 laptop **2** mug **3** surfing **4** looking **5** world

Exercise 6: Read and copy

This exercise reviews spellings previously learnt. The students should complete this task individually and then with a partner, check each other's work. To check learning, using an OHT/IWB, get students to pronounce the words they have copied.

Exercise 7: Read, say and check

Follow the usual procedure.

Answers

1 for	**2** fur	**3** far	**4** tar	**5** tore	**6** Turk	**7** burn
8 born	**9** world	**10** Hamburg	**11** wore	**12** whirl		
13 girl	**14** word	**15** church	**16** surf	**17** surfing		
18 turf	**19** first	**20** turban	**21** turning	**22** her		
23 herb	**24** burning	**25** working	**26** turning			
27 lurk	**28** fork					

Exercise 8: Read, then listen and check

Follow the usual procedure.

Answers

1st = first   @ = at   & = and   £ = pounds
+ = plus   www = World Wide Web   .com = dot com

&   .com   +   1st   @   £   www

surf the net	boy and girl
world wide web	English words
turn up	Turkish coffee
turn down	Word program
her skirt	yes, sir
his shirt	no, sir
my fur coat	please, sir
your sock	go first, sir

Closure

Learn the meaning of the words for clothes in the dry cleaning list in Exercise 6: *shirt, skirt, pants, frock/dress, coat, waistcoat, T-shirt* and *top*.

38

Objectives

By the end of the lesson, students should be able to:

- associate and read *c* as /s/ before *e* and *i* in capitals and lower case in a variety of typefaces, in words of one or two syllables;

- demonstrate recognition and production of previously learnt letters, letter combinations and words.

Adaptations

Faster/mixed-ability classes	Directed self-study
As in previous units, you could start with Exercise 3 as a reading test, and go back to the earlier exercises only if necessary.	Go over the pronunciation of *c* in the contexts covered in this unit (see the Objectives). You could use words from the first two sections of Exercise 1 for this. On the basis of their performance in this, tell student(s) which exercises to do. Remind them that they can replay the CD, or pause it, if they wish.

Words for revision
(also available as flashcards)

bird	blur	burn	burning	burst	church
curl	first	flirt	fur	girl	Hamburg
her	herb	lurk	shirt	sir	skirt
spur	stir	surf	surfing	swirl	tore
turban	turf	Turk	turn	turning	whirl
word	wore	work	working	world	worm
worst					

New letters/words for this lesson
(also available as flashcards)

~ce /s/	ce~ /se/	ci~ /sɪ/		
ace	cement	cent	centigrade	centigram
central	cert	certain	choice	cinema
circus	cite	citrus	civic	civil
cycling	dice	face	fake	fleece
force	ice	ice cream	Kent	kite
mice	Mike	nice	pace	peace
place	plaice	price	race	rake
rice	slice	space	spice	spike
trace	twice	vice	voice	

Introduction

Write words from the revision list on the board/IWB (or use flashcards or an OHT). Choose between these activities:
- **students listen and repeat selected words**
- **designated students read out words**

Exercise 1: Read and say

Exploit the visual. Explain that the unit focuses on the letter *c* as /s/. Follow the normal procedure.

Exercise 2: Listen and tick

Follow the usual procedure.

Answers

Exercise 3: Trace and write

Follow the usual procedure. Check the ascenders and descenders.

Exercise 4: Read and label

Follow the usual procedure. Point out that *cent* means 100.

Answers

1 centimetre **2** century **3** centigrams **4** centigrade
5 centipede

Exercise 5: Find the new words and circle them

This is the first time students have done this type of exercise. Therefore, take care in explaining what to do. If the matter arises, point out that *corn* starts with /k/ because the next letter is *o*. Ask them to find a new word and elicit the word they have found. On an OHT/IWB, circle this word. Tell the students to find other new words and do the same.

Students work individually to circle the words. Set a time limit. Students can then compare their answers with a partner, who may be able to help them find any words they have missed. As each student will have slightly different problems with this exercise, delay further feedback (see Closure).

Answers

	Japan	rice, soyabeans, fish, seafood, seaweed
	China	rice, wheat, beans, pork
	USA	wheat, corn (maize), rice, beef, pork, chicken, turkey, milk
	UK	wheat, oats, chicken, lamb, pork, beef, milk, eggs, cheese

Exercise 6: Read, then listen and check

Follow the usual procedure. Point out that *c* is /k/ (the so-called 'hard' *k*) before *u*.

Answers

cent i grade	centigrade
cent i gram	centigram
cy cling	cycling
cir cus	circus
cer tain	certain

Exercise 7: Read, say and check

Follow the usual procedure.

Answers

a nice ice cream	no cycling	ten centigrade
ten cents each	yes, it's certain	four grams of rice
the space race	a French circus	the marketplace

Exercise 8: Dictation

As a variation, you can do this as a 'wall' dictation.
- Put a copy of the five words in the dictation on a wall in the classroom that everyone can get to.
- Divide the class into twos (or threes, if numbers dictate this).
- One partner/group member goes to the wall and memorizes the first word.
- He/she goes back and whispers the word to his/her partner/group.
- Both/all write it down.
- The other partner/another group member then goes to the wall, memorizes the next word and returns to whisper it to the other(s).
- Both/all write it down.
- And so on with all five words.
- Then they can go and look at the 'master' version on the wall and correct any mistakes (in a different colour).

Monitor throughout. Rules:
- No shouting the answers from the wall!
- No taking pens and paper to the wall!

Answers

1 voice	V-O-I-C-E	voice
2 certain	C-E-R-T-A-I-N	certain
3 cinema	C-I-N-E-M-A	cinema
4 price	P-R-I-C-E	price
5 twice	T-W-I-C-E	twice

Closure

Ask students to find out the meanings of the food-related words from Exercise 5 which they did not know.

Objectives

By the end of the lesson, students should be able to:

- read words ending in *~er* with:
  - double consonants, e.g., *pepper;*
  - consonant clusters, e.g., *farmer;*
  - double vowels, e.g., *sleeper;*
- pronounce *~er* as a schwa (/ə/) (Note: there is no need to explain the word *schwa*.)

Adaptations

Faster/mixed-ability classes	Directed self-study
Start with Exercise 3 as a reading test, and go back to the earlier exercises only if necessary. Make sure that students do not pronounce the *r*. Otherwise, complete Exercise 3 as a trace and write activity.	Go over the pronunciation of *~er* in the contexts covered in this unit (see the Objectives). Make sure that the *r* is not pronounced. Tell student(s) which exercises to do. Remind them that they can replay the CD, or pause it, if they wish.

Notes on new sounds

As noted in the objectives, *~er* in this position is /ə/ (schwa). This is the first time this sound has been taught.

Words for revision
(also available as flashcards)

ace	cement	cent	centi	centigrade
centigram	central	cert	certain	choice
cinema	circus	cite	citrus	civic
civil	cycling	dice	face	fake
fleece	force	ice	ice cream	Kent
kite	mice	Mike	nice	pace
peace	place	plaice	price	race
rake	rice	slice	space	spice
spike	trace	twice	vice	voice

New letters/words for this lesson
(also available as flashcards)

~er /ə/

banker	beefburger	better	bigger	boiler
border	browser	burger	butter	copper
farmer	fatter	hammer	hotter	letter
litter	manner	matter	order	pepper
pointer	power	printer	rubber	scanner
shower	singer	sleeper	sneaker	spammer
speaker	steamer	swimmer	tipper	toaster
trainer	waiter	winner	worker	

Introduction

Write selected words from the revision list on the board/IWB (or use flashcards or an OHT). Choose between these activities:

- **students listen and repeat selected words**
- **designated students read out words**

Exercise 1: Read and say

Exploit the visual. Explain that the unit focuses on the letters *~er* at the end of words. Teach the *schwa* (/ə/) – but do not explain it. With this in mind, follow the normal procedure. However, as this is a long version of this exercise, you might like to break off after section three, do Exercise 3, then come back and complete Exercise 1.

> **Transcript** 🔊 **4.21** (3 mins, 7 secs)
>
> 1 big 2 bigger 3 hot 4 hotter 5 win
> 6 winner
>
> 1 pep 2 pepper 3 rub 4 rubber 5 fat
> 6 fatter 7 sing 8 singer 9 bank 10 banker
>
> 1 better 2 letter 3 pepper 4 hammer
> 5 spammer 6 manner 7 matter 8 planner
> 9 shower 10 rubber 11 butter 12 hotter
> 13 copper 14 bigger 15 burger 16 winner
> 17 tipper 18 singer 19 heater 20 worker
> 21 waiter
>
> 1 butter 2 better 3 banker 4 spammer
> 5 shower 6 planner 7 manner 8 winner 9 singer
> 10 pepper 11 copper 12 tipper 13 burger
> 14 bigger 15 letter 16 worker 17 hotter
> 18 waiter 19 hammer 20 rubber 21 matter
>
> 1 sleeper 2 litter 3 waiter 4 speaker 5 toaster
> 6 swimmer 7 steamer 8 trainer 9 sneaker
> 10 browser 11 farmer 12 boiler 13 border
> 14 pointer 15 scanner 16 printer 17 power
> 18 order

Exercise 2: Listen and tick

Follow the usual procedure.

Answers

winner	worker	sing	planner	rubber	pepper
manner					
butter	letter	burger	heater	spammer	better
pepper					

Exercise 3: Trace and write

Follow the usual procedure. Check the ascenders and descenders.

Exercise 4: Read and label

Follow the usual procedure.

Answers

1 red pepper   **2** black pepper   **3** butter   **4** beefburger
5 hammer   **6** speaker   **7** printer   **8** scanner

Exercise 5: Find and circle words from Unit 39

Follow the usual procedure. Use this exercise as the Closure.

Answers

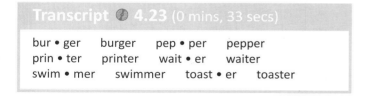

Exercise 6: Read, say and check

Follow the usual procedure.

bur • ger	burger	pep • per	pepper
prin • ter	printer	wait • er	waiter
swim • mer	swimmer	toast • er	toaster

Exercise 7: Read, then listen and check

With the students' books closed, dictate two or three of the phrases. Students open their books and check.

a copper hammer	toast and butter
a power shower	more pepper, please
printer and scanner	a shower of rain
send me a letter	
a web browser	
a bigger beefburger	

Closure

Use Exercise 5 as the Closure. It consolidates the learning of the unit. Ask students to circle the words from the unit, then ask them to read them out.

40   E E R   E A R   E R E

Objectives

By the end of the lesson, students should be able to:

- ■ recognize and read ~eer as /ɪə/;
- ■ recognize and read selected words where ~ear is /ɪə/;
- ■ recognize and read ~ere as /ɪə/;
- ■ demonstrate recognition and production of previously learnt letters, letter combinations and words.

Adaptations

Faster/mixed-ability classes	Directed self-study
Start with Exercise 4 as a reading test, and go back to the earlier exercises only if necessary. Otherwise, complete Exercise 4 as a trace and write activity and work through the rest of the unit.	Go over the pronunciation of ~eer, ~ear and ~ere in the contexts covered in this unit (see the Objectives). Use Exercise 4 as a reading test for this. Tell student(s) which exercises to do. Remind them that they can replay the CD, or pause it, if they wish.

Words for revision
(also available as flashcards)

banker	beefburger	better	bigger	boiler
border	browser	burger	butter	copper
farmer	fatter	hammer	hotter	letter
litter	manner	matter	order	pepper
pointer	power	printer	rubber	scanner
shower	singer	sleeper	sneaker	spammer
speaker	steamer	swimmer	tipper	toaster
trainer	waiter	winner	worker	

New letters/words for this lesson
(also available as flashcards)

eer /ɪə/   ear /ɪə/   ere /ɪə/

beard	cheer	cheering	clear	dear	deer	ear
earring	fear	gear	hearing	here	jeer	near
peer	rear	sneer	spear	tear	we're	year

Introduction

Write selected words from the revision list on the board/IWB (or use flashcards or an OHT). Choose between these activities:

- • **students listen and repeat selected words**
- • **designated students read out words**

Exercise 1: Read and say

Exploit the visual. Explain that the unit focuses on three ways to spell one sound (/ɪə/). The first four letter combinations in the first section revise previously learnt contrasting vowels to /ɪə/. Follow the normal procedure.

Transcript 4.25 (2 mins, 20 secs)

1 ar **2** ir **3** ur **4** er **5** eer **6** ear **7** ere

1 deer **2** cheer **3** ear **4** near **5** here **6** we're

1 deer **2** peer **3** cheer **4** jeer **5** queer **6** sneer
7 dear **8** fear **9** gear **10** hear **11** near **12** rear
13 tear **14** year **15** beard **16** clear **17** spear
18 here **19** we're **20** earring **21** hearing

1 deer **2** dear **3** hear **4** here **5** gear **6** jeer
7 year **8** near **9** we're **10** clear **11** cheer
12 queer **13** sneer **14** beard **15** peer
16 tear **17** rear **18** ear **19** spear **20** hearing
21 fear

Exercise 2: Number from 1–7

Follow the usual procedure.

Answers

Transcript 4.26 (0 mins, 29 secs)

1 year **2** fear **3** cheer **4** here **5** dear **6** we're
7 near

Exercise 3: Listen and tick

Follow the usual procedure.

Answers

Transcript 4.27 (0 mins, 45 secs)

clear	cheer	sneer	year	queer	jeer	earring
far	spur	board	poor	tear	fear	your

Exercise 4: Trace and write

Follow the usual procedure. Check the ascenders and descenders.

Exercise 5: Read and label

Follow the usual procedure.

Answers

1 ear   **2** deer   **3** spear   **4** beard   **5** gear

Exercise 6: Read, then listen and check.

Follow the usual procedure. The three illustrations following this exercise are not on the CD. You could ask volunteers to read the illustrations.

Answers

Transcript 🎵 4.28 (1 min, 15 secs)

1 far   **2** fear   **3** fur   **4** fame   **5** here   **6** her
7 hark   **8** get   **9** grade   **10** gear   **11** jar   **12** jeer
13 dear   **14** date   **15** queen   **16** queer   **17** clench
18 clear   **19** yard   **20** yet   **21** year   **22** your
23 store   **24** stir   **25** steer   **26** star   **27** beard
28 bard   **29** word

Exercise 7: Number the words, then listen and check

Follow the usual procedure.

Answers

Transcript 🎵 4.29 (1 min, 48 secs)

1 = *ear* in *near*   **2** = *ir* in *first*
3 = *ar* in *park*   **4** = *or* in *born*

farm 3	gear 1	burn 2	lawn 4
flirt 2	hard 3	year 1	bird 2
worst 2	jaw 4	bark 3	cheer 1
fork 4	her 2	surf 2	skirt 2
near 1	here 1	queer 1	start 3
far 3	harp 3	sir 2	floor 4
fear 1	chart 3	store 4	dear 1
four 4	shirt 2	rear 1	world 2
girl 2	clear 1	card 3	we're 1

Exercise 8: Read, then listen and check

Follow the usual procedure. Note the *r* pronounced in *we hear it's near* and *cheering and booing*.

Transcript 🎵 4.30 (0 mins, 50 secs)

it's near here	steer clear	top gear
we hear it's near	cheer, don't jeer	stop here
We're here!	cheering and booing	don't stop here
I can hear her	please pay here	a brown beard

Closure

Use the final illustration, the car park notice. Ask students to read it out. Using an OHT/IWB, point to each word in turn, pause, then ask a student to read it. Finally, everybody reads it together.

41 A I R ~ A R E

Objectives

By the end of the lesson, students should be able to:

- recognize and read *air* as /eə/;
- recognize and read *~are* as /eə/ when preceded by a consonant or consonant cluster;
- demonstrate recognition and production of previously learnt letters, letter combinations and words.

Adaptations

Faster/mixed-ability classes	Directed self-study
You could start with Exercise 2 as a reading test, and go back to Exercise 1 only if necessary. Otherwise, begin at Exercise 4.	Go over the pronunciation of *air* and *~are* in the contexts covered in this unit (see the Objectives). You could start with Exercise 2 as a reading test. Tell student(s) which exercises to do. Remind them that they can replay the CD, or pause it, if they wish.

Notes on new sounds

The diphthong /eə/ is easily confused with the pure vowel /ɜː/ as in *her*.

Words for revision
(also available as flashcards)

beard	cheer	cheering	clear	dear	deer
ear	earring	fear	gear	hearing	here
jeer	near	peer	rear	sneer	spear
tear	we're	year			

New letters/words for this lesson
(also available as flashcards)

air /eə/   ~are /eə/

airfare	airport	armchair	bare	care	chair
dairy	dare	fair	fairy	fare	flare
glare	hair	hairy	hare	mare	pair
rare	scare	share	spare	square	stair
stairs					

Introduction

Write words from the revision list on the board/IWB (or use flashcards or an OHT). Choose between these activities:
- students listen and repeat selected words
- designated students read out words

Exercise 1: Read and say

Exploit the visual. Explain that the unit focuses on two ways to spell one sound (/eə/). The first four letter combinations in the first section revise previously learnt contrasting vowels to /eə/. Follow the normal procedure.

Transcript 🄳 4.31 (2 mins, 36 secs)

1 a **2** ai **3** ar **4** ear **5** er **6** ur **7** air **8** are

1 air **2** pair **3** care **4** square

1 air **2** fair **3** hair **4** chair **5** stair **6** dairy
7 fairy **8** hairy **9** airport **10** bare **11** care
12 dare **13** fare **14** hare **15** mare **16** rare
17 flare **18** glare **19** scare **20** square **21** share
22 spare

1 fair **2** mare **3** hare **4** hair **5** hairy **6** chair
7 share **8** flare **9** fairy **10** dare **11** dairy **12** air
13 fare **14** airfare **15** airport **16** bare **17** care
18 scare **19** square **20** stair **21** glare

Exercise 2: Number from 1–7

Follow the usual procedure.

Answers

Transcript 🄳 4.32 (0 mins, 31 secs)

1 rare **2** glare **3** fair **4** dare **5** air **6** square
7 hair

Exercise 3: Listen and tick

Follow the usual procedure.

Answers

fair	car	pair	her	bar	flare	stain
dare	fair	square	glaze	shave	chair	scar

Exercise 4: Trace and write

Follow the usual procedure. Check the ascenders and descenders.

Exercise 5: Read and label

Follow the usual procedure.

Answers

1 chair **2** armchair **3** square **4** stairs **5** brown hair

Exercise 6: Find and circle the words

Ask students to work on their own or with a partner to identify the words and the total number of times the words appear alone, or in another word, e.g., *air* in *Finnair*. Then elicit the words that appear. Settle any disputes with an OHT/IWB already completed.

Answers

Exercise 7: Read, say and check

Follow the usual procedure. However, encourage the sounding of the *r* between vowels. A good contrast is how you say *hair* and *hairy*.

1 fur **2** fear **3** far **4** fair **5** four **6** airfare
7 ferry **8** fairy **9** star **10** stir **11** stair **12** stare
13 bore **14** bar **15** bare **16** bird **17** scar
18 skirt **19** scare **20** her **21** hair **22** hungry
23 hairy **24** round **25** square **26** part **27** port
28 pair

Exercise 8: Read, then listen and check

Follow the usual procedure.

a dairy farm	airfare	it's not fair
pairwork	rail fare	that's my chair
a square box	bus fare	it's not a spare chair

Exercise 9: Dictation

Follow the usual procedure.

Answers

1 air fare	A-I-R F-A-R-E	airfare
2 air port	A-I-R P-O-R-T	airport
3 pair work	P-A-I-R-W-O-R-K	pairwork
4 a spare chair	A S-P-A-R-E C-H-A-I-R	a spare chair

Closure

Ask students to learn the meaning of the words in Exercise 5.

42 | E W U E

Objectives

By the end of the lesson, students should be able to:

- recognize and read *ew* and *ue* as /uː/ or /juː/, according to context;
- demonstrate recognition and production of previously learnt letters, letter combinations and words;
- order words alphabetically.

Adaptations

Faster/mixed-ability classes	Directed self-study
You could start by selecting key words from Exercise 1, section six to read as a test, and do the whole of Exercise 1 only if necessary. Otherwise, begin at Exercise 3.	Check the pronunciation of *ew* and *ue* in the contexts covered in this unit (see the new letters/words given below). Tell student(s) which exercises to do. Remind them that they can replay the CD, or pause it, if they wish.

Words for revision
(also available as flashcards)

air	airfare	airport	armchair	brew	care
chair	dairy	dare	fair	fairy	fare
flare	glare	hair	hairy	hare	mare
pair	rare	scare	share	spare	square
stair	stairs				

New letters/words for this lesson
(also available as flashcards)

The two spellings in this unit can each represent /uː/ or /juː/, depending on the sound that precedes them. Therefore, they have been grouped below to reflect this (as they are in the Course Book). It is suggested that you present the words in these groups before mixing them.

ew /uː/	ue /uː/					
blew	blue	brew	chew	chewing	clue	crew
drew	flew	flue	glue	grew	sue	true

ew /juː/	ue /juː/					
cue	dew	due	few	fewer	new	
newer	pew	queue	queuing	stew	stewing	

Introduction

Write selected words from the revision list on the board/IWB (or use flashcards or an OHT). Choose between these activities:

- **students listen and repeat selected words**
- **designated students read out words**

Exercise 1: Read and say

Note that the words are carefully grouped.

- In sections one and two, *ew* and *ue* are pronounced /uː/.
- In sections three and four, *ew* and *ue* are pronounced /juː/.
- In section three, note that /juː/ is introduced by *y*, then *oo*, followed by *you*.
- In sections five and six, the two sounds are mixed.

As it is a long exercise, vary the presentation. For ideas, look back at the notes for Exercise 1 in Unit 25.

There are several examples of *w* being pronounced when a written *w* is between vowels, e.g., *fewer, newer* and *stewing*. Compare with the *r* pronounced between vowels. Exploit the visual. Draw students' attention to the word *shoe* that follows the plus (+) sign in section one. It is an important word containing the target vowel of the unit, but spelt in an exceptional way. Play the CD for the first two sections. Students repeat after the CD. When you get to section three, draw students' attention to the change from /uː/ to /juː/. Build up the sound /juː/ carefully for this section. Play the CD for sections three and four. Point out that in the word *queue*, *qu* is pronounced /k/ not /kw/. Follow the normal procedure for the remaining sections.

Transcript ⊚ 4.37 (3 mins, 33 secs)

1 o **2** oo **3** too **4** crew **5** flew **6** blue **7** sue **8** shoe

1 blew **2** brew **3** crew **4** chew **5** drew **6** flew **7** grew **8** sue **9** blue **10** clue **11** flue **12** glue **13** true

1 y **2** oo **3** you **4** few **5** new

1 dew **2** few **3** new **4** pew **5** stew **6** fewer **7** newer **8** stewing **9** due **10** cue **11** queue

1 oo **2** you **3** sue **4** new **5** flew **6** few **7** flue **8** cue **9** crew **10** clue **11** chew **12** grew **13** glue **14** dew **15** due **16** shoe **17** blew **18** pew **19** clue **20** queue **21** stew **22** fewer **23** true

1 zoom **2** bloom **3** blue **4** blew **5** sue **6** soon **7** stew **8** you **9** few **10** fewer **11** roof **12** flew **13** too **14** stool **15** true **16** newer **17** chewing **18** queuing **19** do **20** dew **21** go **22** grew

Exercise 2: Listen and tick

Follow the usual procedure.

Answers

Transcript 🔊 4.38 (0 mins, 48 secs)

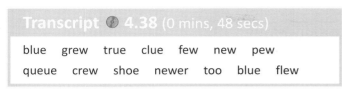

blue   grew   true   clue   few   new   pew

queue   crew   shoe   newer   too   blue   flew

Exercise 3: Trace and write

Follow the usual procedure. Check the ascenders.

Exercise 4: Find and circle the words

Follow the usual procedure.

Answers

Exercise 5: Read, then listen and check

Follow the usual procedure.

Transcript 🔊 4.39 (0 mins, 34 secs)

too   blue   you   stew   shoe

pair   re   repair   ware   be   Beware!

Exercise 6: Add the key words, then listen and check.

This is an exercise revising alphabetical order. Follow the same procedure as for Unit 35, Exercise 6.

Answers

Transcript 🔊 4.40 (2 mins, 4 secs)

a about am **an** and & at @ be been bit born but by can count day did do **doing** don't down drink each eat English first **for** from get go going got had he her here Hi him how if I **in** it just let lot may me mean morning much must near nice **no** not now OK on or out please pound read room saw say see seen **she** shop so soon than that **the** them this too up us we went we're when **which** while with won't yes you your

Exercise 7: Dictation

Follow the usual procedure.

Answers

Transcript 🔊 4.41 (1 min, 25 secs)

1 air crew	A-I-R C-R-E-W	air crew
2 shoe repair	S-H-O-E R-E-P-A-I-R	shoe repair
3 new blue shoes	N-E-W B-L-U-E S-H-O-E-S	new blue shoes
4 just a few	J-U-S-T A F-E-W	just a few

Closure

Ask students to find out the meanings of these words from Exercise 4: *care, fish, fishing, cycle, repair* and *wait.*

43 ~ E L L   ~ I L L

Objectives

By the end of the lesson, students should be able to:

- recognize and read *~ell*, *~ill*, *~all* and *~ull* with the correct vowels;
- demonstrate recognition and production of previously learnt letters, letter combinations and words.

Adaptations

Faster/mixed-ability classes	Directed self-study
As in previous units, you could start with Exercise 2 as a test, and go back to Exercise 1 only if necessary.	Go over the pronunciation of the target letters. Vowels should be distinct. Tell student(s) which exercises to do. Remind them that they can replay the CD, or pause it, if they wish.

Notes on new sounds

The /l/ sound here is at the end of a syllable. Double-*l* is the so-called *dark l*, articulated using the velum, in contrast to the *light l*, which is when /l/ occurs at the beginning of a word in RP. Some students may pronounce a light *l* in place of a dark *l*.

Words for revision
(also available as flashcards)

blew	blue	brew	chew	chewing	clue
crew	cue	dew	drew	due	few
fewer	flew	flue	glue	grew	new
newer	pew	queue	queuing	stew	stewing
sue	true				

New letters/words for this lesson
(also available as flashcards)

~ell /el/   ~ill /ɪl/   ~all /ɔːl/   ~ull /ʊl/

all	ball	bell	bill	bull	call	cell
chill	cill	ell	fall	fell	fill	full
grill	hall	hill	ill	kill	mall	mill
pill	pull	quill	sell	shell	silly	skill
small	smell	spell	squall	stall	still	tall
tell	till	villa	wall	well	will	

Introduction

Write selected words from the revision list on the board/IWB (or use flashcards or an OHT). Choose between these activities:

- **students listen and repeat selected words**
- **individual designated students read out words**

Exercise 1: Read and say

Note that the words are carefully grouped.

- Section one introduces the sounds of the four letter combinations.
- Section two is composed of words incorporating *~ell*.
- Section three is composed of words incorporating *~ill*.

- Section four builds up the sound of *~all* before exemplifying words incorporating *~all*.
- Section five builds up the sound of *~ull* before exemplifying words incorporating *~ull*.
- Section six mixes the four letter combinations.

Exploit the visual. Play the CD section by section. Students repeat after the CD.

Transcript 🔊 4.42 (3 mins, 0 secs)

1 bell   **2** bill   **3** ball   **4** bull

1 ell   **2** bell   **3** cell   **4** fell   **5** hell   **6** sell   **7** tell   **8** well   **9** shell   **10** smell   **11** spell

1 ill   **2** bill   **3** cill   **4** fill   **5** hill   **6** kill   **7** mill   **8** pill   **9** quill   **10** till   **11** still   **12** skill   **13** will   **14** grill   **15** chill   **16** silly   **17** villa

1 or   **2** all   **3** ball   **4** call   **5** fall   **6** hall   **7** mall   **8** tall   **9** wall   **10** small   **11** stall   **12** squall

1 ull   **2** bull   **3** full   **4** pull

1 all   **2** ill   **3** bill   **4** ball   **5** bell   **6** bull   **7** fill   **8** fall   **9** fell   **10** full   **11** pill   **12** pull   **13** spell   **14** spill   **15** small   **16** smell   **17** skill   **18** grill   **19** well   **20** wall   **21** will   **22** hill   **23** hall   **24** hell

Exercise 2: Listen and tick

Follow the usual procedure.

Answers

Transcript 🔊 4.43 (0 mins, 38 secs)

ill	ball	bill	bull	will	well	full
till	tell	hill	pull	small	spell	skill

Exercise 3: Trace and write

Follow the usual procedure. Check *m's* and *w's*.

Exercise 4: Read and label

Follow the usual procedure.

Answers

1 shell **2** wall **3** bell **4** pills **5** bull

Exercise 5: Find and circle *ll* words

Set this activity by eliciting from the students if they play or like football, etc. This exercise can be used as the Closure. Students work individually and then compare results. Monitor. Show the answers on an OHT/IWB.

Answers

baseball — Toronto Blue Jays
football — Chelsea
football — Aston Villa
American football — New York Jets
rugby football — Bradford Bulls
football — Blackburn Rovers
American football — Dallas Cowboys
basketball — Atlanta Hawks

Exercise 6: Break down the words into syllables

In this new exercise, explain and demonstrate what to do using an OHT/IWB. Students can work in partners or individually. Ask them to write out the answers. Allow sufficient time to complete the task. Monitor and correct thoroughly as the students work.

Answers

Brad•ford   Black•burn Ro•vers   Chel•sea FC
base•ball   rug•by   cow•boy   As•ton Vil•la
At•lan•ta Hawks

Exercise 7: Read, say and check

A hidden pronunciation point in saying these words is the difference between *ll* as a final sound (a dark *l*) and *ll* between two vowels (a light *l*). Follow the usual procedure with this in mind.

Exercise 8: Dictation

Follow the usual procedure.

Answers

Closure

Use Exercise 5 for this phase, as it consolidates learning.

44 ~IGHT OUGHT

Objectives

By the end of the lesson, students should be able to:

- recognize and read ~*ight*, ~*ought*, ~*aught* and ~*eight* with the correct vowels;

- read the target letter combinations in a variety of typefaces;

- demonstrate recognition and production of previously learnt letters, letter combinations and words.

Adaptations

Faster/mixed-ability classes	Directed self-study
As in previous units, you could start with Exercise 2 as a test, and go back to Exercise 1 only if necessary.	Make sure students understand that the letter *g* is not pronounced in these words. Vowels should be distinct. Tell student(s) which exercises to do. Remind them that they can replay the CD, or pause it, if they wish.

Words for revision
(also available as flashcards)

all	ball	bell	bill	bull	call	cell
chill	cill	ell	fall	fell	fill	full
grill	hall	hill	ill	kill	mall	mill
pill	pull	quill	sell	shell	silly	skill
small	smell	spell	squall	stall	still	tall
tell	till	villa	wall	well	will	

New letters/words for this lesson
(also available as flashcards)

~ight /aɪt/	ought /ɔːt/	~aught /ɔːt/	~eight /eɪt/
ate	bought	bright	brought	caught
eighteen	eighty	fight	flight	fought
fright	height	high	light	midnight
might	neighbour	night	nought	ought
right	sigh	sight	sign	slight
tight	weigh	weight		

Introduction

Write selected words from the revision list on the board/IWB (or use flashcards or an OHT). Choose between these activities:

- **students listen and repeat selected words**
- **designated students read out words**

Exercise 1: Read and say

Make it clear to the students that some letters are *silent*. As Exercise 1 is long, vary the procedure as you have done before. The last section covers the same words as the section before. It can be left out if students have clearly learnt the spellings, or you can break before the last section, do Exercise 2 and then go back and do the last section of Exercise 1.

The words are grouped as follows:

- Section one establishes the vowel sound /aɪ/ and goes on to associate it with ~*ight*.
- Section two is composed of words incorporating ~*ight*. *High* and *sigh* have been included to show that ~*igh* represents the same vowel sound. Note the inclusion of *height* – a different spelling for the same vowel.
- Section three establishes the vowel sound in ~*ought* and ~*aught*.
- Section four mixes the spellings covered so far and contains examples of the two vowels associated with ~*eight* – *height* and *weight*.
- Section five focuses on the contrast between the vowels in ~*ought*/~*aught* and ~*eight*.

Play the CD section by section. Students repeat after the CD.

Transcript 4.46 (2 mins, 49 secs)

1 I   2 my   3 ite   4 yte   5 ight

1 fight   2 light   3 might   4 night   5 right   6 sight
7 tight   8 bright   9 flight   10 fright   11 slight
12 midnight   13 high   14 sigh   15 height   16 sign

1 or   2 sort   3 fort   4 fought   5 caught   6 ate
7 eight   8 eight   9 wait   10 weight

1 fight   2 fought   3 taught   4 tight   5 nought
6 night   7 light   8 right   9 bright   10 flight
11 fright   12 caught   13 midnight   14 ought
15 bought   16 height   17 weight   18 sigh   19 sight
20 sign   21 might   22 eight   23 brought   24 high
25 neighbour

1 ought   2 bought   3 fought   4 nought   5 brought
6 caught   7 taught   8 weight   9 eight   10 eighteen
11 weigh   12 neighbour

Exercise 2: Listen and tick

Follow the usual procedure.

Answers

Transcript 🎧 **4.47** (0 mins, 44 secs)
light   fright   might   brought   weight   eight caught
height   white   late   high   sign   say   fight

Exercise 3: Tick (✓) the same sounds and cross (✗) the different sounds

Follow the procedure given for Exercise 4 in Unit 35. Using the example to explain, emphasize it is the vowel sound (not the consonants) that the students must judge as the same or different in each pair. Students should do this individually. Allow two minutes. Monitor. Then, with a partner, students can check each other's work. Feed back the answers using an OHT/IWB with the word pairs ticked or crossed. Draw attention to the visual on the right. It is not connected with the exercise, but may be quickly read and repeated aloud.

Answers
1 ✓   2 ✗   3 ✓   4 ✓   5 ✗   6 ✓   7 ✗   8 ✗

Exercise 4: Trace and write

Follow the usual procedure. Check the ascenders and descenders.

Exercise 5: Find the different word

Answers

night	night	*night*	(*might*)	NIGHT
right	(night)	right	*Right*	*right*
(brought)	bought	bought	*bought*	bought
weight	weight	WEIGHT	weight	(weigh)
CAUGHT	(taught)	*caught*	caught	caught

Exercise 6: Read and copy

Exploit the visual. Remind students they do not need to understand every word. Follow the usual procedure (see the notes for Exercise 6, Unit 37).

Exercise 7: Read, then listen and check

Follow the usual procedure.

Transcript 🎧 **4.48** (0 mins, 51 secs)		
a night flight	drive on the right	eighty-eight
a midnight flight	please sign here	eighteen forty
day and night	I bought eight	a great weight
goodnight	a bright light	a great height

Closure

Use flashcards of words from Exercise 1 to quickly consolidate learning – don't allow too much time for this. Students either read individually, or as a class.

Objectives

By the end of the lesson, students should be able to:

- recognize and read *u~e* as /uː/ or /juː/ + *consonant*, according to the preceding consonant;

- demonstrate recognition and production of previously learnt letters, letter combinations and words.

Adaptations

Faster/mixed-ability classes	Directed self-study
As in previous units, you could start with Exercise 3 as a test, and go back to Exercise 1 only if necessary.	Check students understand how to do Exercise 5. Go over the pronunciation of the target letters. Vowels should be distinct. Tell student(s) which exercises to do. Remind them that they can replay the CD, or pause it, if they wish.

Words for revision

(also available as flashcards)

ate	bought	bright	brought	caught	eighteen
eighty	fight	flight	fought	fright	height
high	light	midnight	might	neighbour	night
nought	ought	right	sigh	sight	sign
slight	tight	weigh	weight		

New letters/words for this lesson

(also available as flashcards)

In this unit, *u~e* can represent /uː/ or /juː/, depending on the sound that precedes it. The words below have been grouped to reflect this (they are grouped in the same way in the Course Book). It is suggested that you present the words in these groups before mixing them.

u~e /juː/

amuse	cube	cute	duke	dune	fuse	June
muse	music	reduce	tube	tune	use	

u~e /uː/

crude	dude	fluke	flute	Luke	lute	prude
prune	rude	rule	ruler			

Introduction

Refer back to Units 25–27 on *a~e*, *i~e* and *o~e*. This unit on *u~e* follows the same lengthening of the first vowel sound when an *e* follows the consonant. For the teacher's information only, in British primary teaching this is often called 'the magic *e*.' However, the underlying rule is not truly the addition of *e*, but is the existence of a vowel-consonant-vowel combination at the end of a word, which results in the lengthening of the first vowel. It happens when other vowels follow a consonant also.

This is an important concept, because it explains the doubling of the consonant in the spelling of some present participles (with *~ing*), comparatives (with *~er*), superlatives with (*~est*) and regular past forms (with *~ed*). So when adding *~ing* to *stop*, we double the *p* to avoid *stoping*, which would mean lengthening the *o* sound, hence we write *stopping*. We also have to double the consonant when we add *~ed* to make it past tense – *stopped*, NOT *stoped*. The same is happening with *big/bigger* and *hot/hottest*. The next unit, Unit 46, shows the doubling of consonants in some other words.

Write selected words from the revision list on the board/IWB (or use flashcards or an OHT). Choose between these activities:
- **students listen and repeat selected words**
- **designated students read out words**

Exercise 1: Read and say

Note that the words are carefully grouped.
- Sections one and two establish the sound /juː/ in *cube*.
- Section three focuses on the effect of adding *e* to *u~*.
- Section four practises *u~e* as /uː/.
- Section five mixes /juː/ and /uː/.

Exploit the visual. Play the CD section by section. Students repeat after the CD.

1 mad **2** made **3** quit **4** quite **5** not **6** note
7 cub **8** cube

1 new **2** few **3** cue **4** cube **5** cub **6** ice cube

1 cub **2** cube **3** cut **4** cute **5** dud **6** dude
7 duck **8** duke **9** dun **10** dune **11** tub
12 tube **13** tun **14** tune **15** us **16** use **17** fuse
18 June **19** muse **20** music **21** amuse **22** reduce

1 rude **2** rule **3** Luke **4** lute **5** flute **6** fluke
7 crude **8** prude **9** prune **10** ruler

1 hop **2** hope **3** wit **4** white **5** lit **6** light
7 Sam **8** same **9** hot **10** hotel **11** us **12** use
13 cut **14** cute **15** luck **16** Luke **17** few **18** due
19 dune **20** duck **21** duke **22** fade **23** hate
24 site **25** sit **26** sight **27** cub **28** club **29** cube
30 fuse **31** music **32** amuse **33** ruler

Exercise 2: Number from 1−5

Follow the usual procedure, but note that there are only five words and the first number has not been marked.

Answers

1 blue **2** Luke **3** too **4** true **5** luck

Exercise 3: Listen and tick

Follow the usual procedure.

Answers

dot pine pane cube tub use cut
flute prune crude fluke fool fuse amuse

Exercise 4: Trace and write

Follow the usual procedure.

Exercise 5: Find the new words and circle them, then listen and check

This exercise can be used as the Closure. It checks how much students have learnt from what has already been covered. (The words covered so far form the vast majority of the exercise.) Words they might not be able to read confidently include: *funny, weather* and *London*.

Give students a reasonable time to complete the task individually. Give help if asked. When everyone is ready, play the CD. Practise *funny, weather* and *London*.

Answers

website inbox e-mail print time 18:10 date 18 June

YouTube iTunes music Toast: burn CDs eBay: buy and sell on the net

My menu Music songs artists blues jazz Podcasts iTunes store

YouTube music funny clips cute kids

Flight tracker Airline British Airways BA003 from New York to London CHECK NOW

world time Hong Kong: 02:10 London: 18:10 New York: 13:10

world weather Hong Kong: cloudy London: storms New York: windy

Exercise 6: Read, then listen and check

Follow the usual procedure.

Answers

1 by **2** buy **3** burn **4** music **5** iTunes
6 YouTube **7** reduce speed now

iTunes music   buy on eBay
tunes from a website sell on eBay
download a tune   a good new rule

a ruler
a new ruler
a new blue ruler

Closure

Use Exercise 5 as the Closure.

46 ~ (T T) L E

Objectives

By the end of the lesson, students should be able to:

- recognize and read *vowel + consonant(s) + le*;
- demonstrate recognition and production of previously learnt letters, letter combinations and words.

Adaptations

Faster/mixed-ability classes	Directed self-study
As in previous units, you could start with Exercise 2 as a test, and go back to Exercise 1 only if necessary.	The pronunciation of *~le* has /ə/ as its first element. This is new. Check students can pronounce it. Tell student(s) which exercises to do. Remind them that they can replay the CD, or pause it, if they wish.

Words for revision
(also available as flashcards)

amuse   crude   cube   cute   dude   duke   dune
fluke   flute   fuse   June   Luke   lute   muse
music   prude   prune   reduce   rude   rule   ruler
tube   tune   use

New letters/words for this lesson
(also available as flashcards)

~(tt)le /əl/   ~(t)le /əl/

able   apple   battle   Beatles   beetle   bible
bottle   bubble   cable   cattle   cradle   cripple
cuddle   dazzle   drizzle   fable   fiddle   gable
giggle   goggle   google   griddle   hobble   kettle
little   middle   muddle   needle   noodle   paddle
puddle   raffle   rifle   ripple   rubble   settle
shuttle   sizzle   table   tattle   title   wobble

Introduction

Write words from the revision list on the board/IWB (or use flashcards or an OHT). Choose between these activities:
- **students listen and repeat selected words**
- **designated students read out words**

Exercise 1: Read and say

Note that the words are carefully grouped.
- Sections one and two focus on *vowel + single consonant + le*.
- Section three contrasts *vowel + single consonant + le* and *vowel + double consonant + le*.
- Section four practises *vowel + double consonant +le*.
- Section five mixes *vowel + single consonant + le* and *vowel + double consonant + le*.

Exploit the visual. Play the CD section by section. Students repeat after the CD.

Transcript 5.6 (3 mins, 12 secs)

1 cab   2 cable   3 tab   4 table   5 bib   6 bible
7 rif   8 rifle

1 able   2 cable   3 fable   4 gable   5 table   6 bible
7 rifle   8 title   9 cradle   10 needle   11 noodle
12 google   13 beetle   14 Beatles

1 gab   2 gable   3 tap   4 apple   5 set   6 settle
7 gig   8 giggle   9 hob   10 hobble   11 mud
12 muddle   13 dazzle

1 apple   2 battle   3 cattle   4 raffle   5 paddle
6 dazzle   7 cripple   8 fiddle   9 giggle   10 little
11 middle   12 ripple   13 sizzle   14 drizzle
15 griddle   16 kettle   17 settle   18 bottle
19 wobble   20 goggle   21 bubble   22 cuddle
23 muddle   24 puddle   25 rubble   26 shuttle

1 table   2 tattle   3 title   4 little   5 rifle   6 middle
7 cattle   8 kettle   9 sizzle   10 shuttle   11 google
12 muddle   13 noodle   14 able   15 apple

Exercise 2: Listen and tick

Follow the usual procedure.

Answers

Transcript 5.7 (0 mins, 39 secs)

table   needle   beat   goggle   puddle   drizzle   cattle

rubber   little   battle   giggle   middle   rifle   noodle

Exercise 3: Trace and write

Follow the usual procedure.

Exercise 4: Read and label

Follow the usual procedure

Answers

1 table   **2** rifle   **3** kettle   **4** bottle   **5** cable

Exercise 5: Find the new words and circle them

This exercise checks how much students have learnt from what has already been covered. However, they may have a small problem with including or omitting *and* in numbers such as 340. Give students a reasonable time to complete the task individually. Give help if asked.

Answers

table 1: baby dept		
sales	this year	next year
kettles	340	310
cradles	290	410
bottles	15,000	14,000

Exercise 6: Read, then listen and check

Follow the usual procedure.

Transcript 🔊 **5.8** (0 mins, 51 secs)

cable TV
google 'noodle'
Apple Mac
puddle in the middle

space shuttle
Apple Records
The Beatles
sizzle on the griddle

a little bit more
a little bottle
a kettle on the table
apple on the table

Exercise 7: Dictation

Follow the usual procedure.

Answers

Transcript 🔊 **5.9** (1 min, 45 secs)

1 bottle in the middle   B-O-T-T-L-E space I-N space T-H-E space M-I-D-D-L-E   bottle in the middle

2 apples on the table   A-P-P-L-E-S space O-N space T-H-E space T-A-B-L-E   apples on the table

3 shuttle bus   S-H-U-T-T-L-E space B-U-S   shuttle bus

4 google and giggle   G-O-O-G-L-E space A-N-D space G-I-G-G-L-E   google and giggle

Exercise 8: Find the words from Unit 46

Use this exercise as the Closure. Follow the usual procedure.

Answers

T	F	F	Q	M	J	A	E	N	T
I	A	D	R	I	Z	Z	L	E	A
T	B	X	G	D	P	L	O	E	B
L	L	P	A	D	D	L	E	D	L
E	E	X	B	L	R	I	F	L	E
A	P	P	L	E	G	R	Z	E	A
B	O	B	E	M	U	D	D	L	E
L	B	O	T	T	L	E	K	M	H
E	L	N	G	I	G	G	L	E	L

Closure

Use Exercise 8 as the Closure.

47 ~OLD ~OULD

Objectives
By the end of the lesson, students should be able to:

- recognize and read ~old as /əʊld/;
- distinguish between ~ould as /ʊd/ in modals and /əʊld/ in other word classes;
- demonstrate recognition and production of previously learnt letters, letter combinations and words.

Adaptations

Faster/mixed-ability classes	Directed self-study
As in previous units, you could start with Exercise 3 as a test of pronunciation and reading, and go back to Exercise 1 only if necessary.	Go over the two vowels involved in the pronunciation of the target letters. Establish that the written *l* in *could, would* and *should* is not pronounced. Point out the two pronunciations of ~*ould* according to word class. Tell student(s) which exercises to do. Remind them that they can replay the CD, or pause it, if they wish.

Notes on new sounds
/l/ in ~*old* and ~*ould* is vocalized by most native speakers, but it is the vowel quality that is important.

Words for revision
(also available as flashcards)

able	apple	battle	Beatles	beetle	bible
bottle	bubble	cable	cattle	cradle	cripple
cuddle	dazzle	drizzle	fable	fiddle	gable
giggle	goggle	google	griddle	hobble	kettle
little	middle	muddle	needle	noodle	paddle
puddle	raffle	rifle	ripple	rubble	settle
shuttle	sizzle	table	tattle	title	wobble

New letters/words for this lesson
(also available as flashcards)

~old /əʊld/		~ould /əʊld/	~ould /ʊd/		
boulder	cold	colder	could	fold	folder
folding	gold	hold	holding	mould	mouldy
old	older	should	shoulder	sold	told
would					

Introduction
This unit is the first to teach two possible phonetic realizations of the same letter combination. It teaches the reading of the vowel in ~old, which is always /əʊ/, and the two pronunciations of ~ould, as /ʊ/ in modals and /əʊ/ in other contexts. The ability to make this distinction correctly is a key objective of the unit. The unit also teaches a homophone for the first time (bolder/boulder).

Write selected words from the revision list on the board/IWB (or use flashcards or an OHT). Choose between these activities:
- **students listen and repeat selected words**
- **designated students read out words**

Exercise 1: Read and say
Note that the words are carefully grouped.
- Sections one and two mix the two spellings of /əʊld/.
- Section three presents ~*ould* as /ɑːd/ in modals.
- Section four mixes /əʊld/ and /ɑːd/.

Establish that in *could, would* and *should*, the written *l* is not pronounced. Then follow the usual procedure. Exploit the visual. Play the CD section by section. Students repeat after the CD.

Transcript 🔊 5.10 (2 mins, 8 secs)

1 odd 2 goal 3 old 4 cold 5 gold 6 older
7 boulder 8 shoulder

1 old 2 bold 3 cold 4 fold 5 gold 6 hold
7 sold 8 told 9 mould 10 older 11 folder
12 colder 13 boulder 14 shoulder

1 good 2 wood 3 could 4 would 5 should

1 cold 2 could 3 sold 4 should 5 shoulder
6 good 7 gold 8 told 9 bold 10 wood
11 would 12 mould 13 hold 14 fold 15 folder
16 older 17 colder 18 bold 19 hood 20 boulder
21 mouldy 22 folding 23 holding

Exercise 2: Number from 1–7

Follow the usual procedure. Then ask different students to read out a word from the list. Say a number and the student says the word.

Answers

1 shoulder	2 older	3 told	4 could	5 should
6 old	7 would			

Exercise 3: Listen and tick

Follow the usual procedure.

Answers

folder   cold   boulder   goal   cod   told   hold

should   word   could   card   would   should

shade

Exercise 4: Tick (✓) the same sounds and cross (✗) the different sounds

Follow the usual procedure, but if students find the exercise difficult, say all the words first with students' pencils down.

Answers

1 ✗   2 ✓   3 ✓   4 ✗   5 ✗   6 ✓   7 ✓   8 ✗

Exercise 5: Trace and write

Remind students that the letter *l* should be slightly taller than *d*. Then follow the usual procedure. Monitor as the students work.

Exercise 6: Read, then listen and check

Follow the usual procedure. After listening to the CD, select (by number) contrasting examples for students to read back.

Answers

1 moon	2 June	3 good	4 would	5 shoot
6 shout	7 shoulder	8 should	9 cold	10 could
11 hood	12 noodle	13 needle	14 bold	
15 bolder	16 boulder	17 fold	18 too	19 tune
20 tub	21 tube	22 told		

old gold coin	ice-cold drink
old shoulder bag	nice cold drink
falling boulders	sold a cold drink
Beware! Falling boulders!	ice-cold drinks sold here

a cold wood
an old wood
a good old wood
an old cold wood

Exercise 7: Find and circle words from Unit 47, then listen and check

Exploit the visual by doing paired practice or a role play of the mini dialogues. Avoid *I'd like* at this stage.

Answers

Waitress:	**Would** you like a hot drink or a **cold** drink?
Customer:	I **would** like a **cold** drink.
Waitress:	**Would** you like ice?
Customer:	Yes, I **would**.

Exercise 8: Find words from Unit 47

Use this exercise as the Closure. Tell students there are ten words containing *ld* and three words which don't contain *ld* but which are in the unit. Follow the usual procedure. Using an OHT/IWB, ask students to read the captions of the pictures to you.

Answers

Closure

Use Exercise 8 as the Closure.

48   T H   T H ~

Objectives

By the end of the lesson, students should be able to:

- recognize and read *th* and *th~* as voiced (/ð/) or unvoiced/voiceless (/θ/);

- realize the initial *th* as voiced (/ð/) only in pronouns and conjunctions (e.g., *than*);

- read numbers (digits) containing *th* (e.g., *three, thirteen* and *thirty*);

- read *thirteenth* and understand it is an ordinal number;

- demonstrate recognition and production of previously learnt letters, letter combinations and words.

Adaptations

Faster/mixed-ability classes	Directed self-study
Start with examples of voiced and unvoiced *th* from Exercise 1 as a test of pronunciation and reading. Do the whole of Exercise 1 only if necessary. Because of the structure of the unit, faster learners should begin with Exercise 2.	Go over the voiced and invoiced *th* sounds to see if learners can distinguish between the two. Tell student(s) which exercises to do. If Exercise 1 is not necessary, begin at Exercise 2. Remind students they can replay the CD, or pause it, if they wish.

Notes on new sounds

Some nationalities find *th* either very difficult or simply embarrassing, confusing the sound with a lisp. Faced with this, unlike native British English speakers, who increasingly opt for *th-fronting* or producing /f/ and /v/ instead of *th*, foreign learners use /s/ and /z/, which is either what they think they are actually hearing, or a way out of making embarrassing noises. Therefore, understanding on the teacher's part is required for learners in this situation.

Words for revision
(also available as flashcards)

boulder	cold	colder	could	fold	folder
folding	gold	hold	holding	mould	mouldy
old	older	should	shoulder	sold	told
would					

New letters/words for this lesson
(also available as flashcards)

th /θ/	th /ð/				
birth	both	breath	breathe	further	gather
maths	mouth	north	soothe	south	teeth
than	thank	that	thaw	them	then
thick	thin	thing	third	thirsty	thirteen
thirty	this	thought	three	thrill	with
youth					

Introduction

This unit teaches two possible phonetic realizations (voiced and unvoiced/voiceless) of the same letter combination – *th*. The ability to make this distinction correctly is a key objective of the unit.

Write selected words from the revision list on the board/IWB (or use flashcards or an OHT). Choose between these activities:

- **students listen and repeat selected words**
- **designated students read out words**

Exercise 1: Read and say

Note that the words are carefully grouped. Sections one, two and five are colour-coded: voiced *th* is red and unvoiced/voiceless *th* is blue.

- Section one contains voiced *th*.
- Sections two, three and four contain unvoiced/voiceless *th*.
- Sections five and six mix the two.

Exploit the visual. This is a long exercise. If desired, break off after section four and do Exercise 4. Then go back and complete Exercise 1. Play the CD section by section. Students repeat after the CD.

Transcript 🔊 5.15 (3 mins, 4 secs)

1 th   2 than   3 that   4 them   5 then   6 this
7 with   8 gather   9 further   10 breathe   11 soothe

1 th   2 th   3 thank   4 thing   5 mouth   6 north

1 thick   2 thin   3 think   4 thing   5 thank   6 three
7 thirteen   8 thirty   9 third   10 thorn   11 thaw
12 thought   13 thirsty   14 thrill

1 mouth   2 south   3 north   4 tooth   5 teeth
6 birth   7 breath   8 youth   9 both   10 maths

1 thin   2 thick   3 this   4 thing   5 than   6 thank
7 breathe   8 breath   9 further   10 birth

1 think   2 thin   3 three   4 teeth   5 thought
6 north   7 south   8 soothe   9 thirty   10 further
11 youth   12 both   13 birth   14 thought   15 this

Exercise 2: Listen and tick

Follow the usual procedure.

Answers

Transcript 🔊 5.16 (0 mins, 50 secs)

than   ten   this   with   soon   thank   three
third   thirsty

too   tooth   teeth   nor   torn   boat   math   birth
nought

Exercise 3: Listen and write the numbers

This is a simple dictation, which also revises writing Arabic numerals. Play the CD to familiarize students with the numbers. Play the CD again, pausing after each prompt to let students write. Then put the answers on the board. Ask students to provide the answers if they are confident.

Answers

Transcript 🔊 5.17 (0 mins, 43 secs)

1 three   2 eight   3 thirteen   4 eighteen   5 thirty
6 eighty   7 thirty-eight

Exercise 4: Trace and write

Follow the usual procedure. Monitor as the students work.

Exercise 5: Read, say and check

Follow the usual procedure.

Transcript 🔊 5.18 (1 min, 7 secs)

1 too   2 tooth   3 tea   4 teeth   5 bought
6 thought   7 fur   8 further   9 porch   10 north
11 out   12 south   13 that   14 gather   15 born
16 birth   17 three   18 third   19 thirty   20 thirsty
21 breath   22 breathe

Exercise 6: Find words from Unit 48, then listen and check

Follow the usual procedure. The road signs do not appear on the audio CD as they are for illustration only.

Answers

Transcript 🔊 5.19 (0 mins, 32 secs)

north   **north**-east   east   **south**-east   **south**
south-west   west   **north**-west

Exercise 7: Find more words from Unit 48, then listen and check

Follow the procedure for Exercise 6. Elicit the words. The students should be able to read every word, with the possible exceptions of *1983* and *Southampton*.

Answers

Transcript 🔊 5.20 (0 mins, 33 secs)

First name: Kathy
Surname: Thatcher
Date of **birth**: 13th June 1983
Place of **birth**: **South**ampton

Exercise 8: Read the key words, then listen and check

Use this exercise as the Closure. Using an OHT/IWB, get students to read the words. When a student gives a really good reading, acknowledge this, and ask him/her to repeat it. Then select other students. If time is limited, select specific words.

Transcript 🔊 5.21 (0 mins, 57 secs)

with   both   birth   date of birth   place of birth
than   thank   that   the   them   this   thing
three   third   thirteen   thirty   thirteenth
can   could   will   would   should   may   might

Closure

Use Exercise 8 as the Closure.

Objectives

By the end of the lesson, students should be able to:

- read the irregular spellings *one* and *two*;
- read regular spellings of /ʌ/, e.g., *gun*;
- read exceptional spellings of /ʌ/, e.g., *son*;
- read and recognize ordinal numbers, including the abbreviated forms (1st, 2nd, 3rd, 4th);
- read and recognize cardinal numbers *thirty, forty* and *fifty*, etc., to *ninety*;
- read and recognize the consonant changes in *twelve/twelfth, five/fifteen/fifty*.

Adaptations

Faster/mixed-ability classes	Directed self-study
Start by taking key examples from section five of Exercise 1 as a test of pronunciation and reading. Do the whole of Exercise 1 only if necessary. Because of the structure of the unit, faster learners should begin with Exercise 2.	Go over the students' recognition of key words from the unit. Tell student(s) which exercises to do. If Exercise 1 is not necessary, begin at Exercise 2. Remind them that they can replay the CD, or pause it, if they wish.

Words for revision
(also available as flashcards)

birth	both	breath	breathe	further	gather
maths	mouth	north	soothe	south	teeth
than	thank	that	thaw	them	then
thick	thin	thing	third	thirsty	thirteen
thirty	this	thought	three	thrill	with
youth					

New letters/words for this lesson
(also available as flashcards)

bun	eighth	eighty	eleventh	fifth	fifty
first	forty	fourth	fun	gun	ninety
ninth	one	rum	second	seventh	seventy
sixth	sixty	son	sun	tenth	third
thirteenth	thirty	to	twelfth	twenty	two
won					

Introduction

This unit covers the exceptional spellings of *one* and *two*, and how cardinal and ordinal numbers, up to one hundred, are written.

Write selected words from the revision list on the board/IWB (or use flashcards or an OHT). Choose between these activities:

- **students listen and repeat selected words**
- **designated students read out words**

Exercise 1: Read and say

Note that the words are carefully grouped.

- Section one establishes the pronunciation of *one*.
- Section two establishes the pronunciation of *two*.
- Section three takes the reading (in word form) numbers to *fifty*. Note that the consonant changes are highlighted in red.
- Section four teaches the full and abbreviated forms of ordinal numbers.
- Section five mixes all the elements of the previous sections.

Exploit the visual. This is a long exercise. If desired, break off after section four and do Exercise 4. Then go back and complete Exercise 1. Play the CD section by section. Students repeat after the CD.

Transcript 🔊 5.22 (3 mins, 29 secs)

1 bun	**2** fun	**3** gun	**4** sun	**5** won	**6** son	**7** one
8 1	**9** come	**10** some				

1 to	**2** too	**3** you	**4** do	**5** queue	**6** two	**7** 2

1 one	**2** two	**3** three	**4** four	**5** five	**6** six
7 seven	**8** eight	**9** nine	**10** ten	**11** eleven
12 twelve	**13** thirteen	**14** fourteen	**15** fifteen
16 sixteen	**17** seventeen	**18** eighteen	**19** nineteen
20 twenty	**21** thirty	**22** forty	**23** fifty

1 first	**2** second	**3** third	**4** fourth	**5** fifth	**6** sixth
7 seventh	**8** eighth	**9** ninth	**10** tenth
11 eleventh	**12** twelfth	**13** thirteenth

1 win	**2** on	**3** won	**4** one	**5** toe	**6** too	**7** top
8 to	**9** two	**10** you	**11** rum	**12** gum	**13** come
14 sum	**15** some	**16** home	**17** son	**18** one
19 two	**20** 2nd	**22** 3rd	**23** 1st	**24** 4th	**25** 9th
26 5th	**27** 12th

Exercise 2: Listen and tick

Follow the usual procedure.

Answers

> **Transcript** 🔊 5.23 (0 mins, 51 secs)
>
> first   thirst   first   fourth   fifth   six   seventh
> eleven   twelfth
>
> thirteen   forty   fifty   sixteen   seventy   eighteen
> ninety   fifteenth   nineteen

Exercise 3: Trace and write

Follow the usual procedure. Monitor as the students work.

Exercise 4: Match the numbers with the spaces

This exercise establishes the connection between the full-length and abbreviated forms of ordinal numbers. Do the first one as an example as this is a new exercise type.

Answers

1 3rd   **2** 10th   **3** 6th   **4** 13th   **5** 9th   **6** 2nd   **7** 12th
8 4th   **9** 11th   **10** 5th   **11** 1st   **12** 8th

Exercise 5: Find the different word

Follow the usual procedure.

third	_third_	_third_	(thirty)	THIRD
fifth	(five)	fifth	_fifth_	fifth
one	one	_one_	ONE	(on)
two	(twin)	two	_two_	TWO
(second)	seventh	seventh	_seventh_	**SEVENTH**

Exercise 6: Fill in the missing numbers

This is a new exercise. Get the students to identify the first missing number (*three*). Tell the students that they should read the whole of each row before beginning it. All the words in row 1 are like *one, two,* etc. All the words in row 2 are like *second, third,* etc. For row 3, the students have to understand that it is odd numbers that are missing. One way of achieving this would be to write row 3 on the board as numerals, with ones that are missing included. Then ask them to look at the written version in row 3 and complete it. See if students can complete row 4 without help. For row 5, point out that *st, nd,* etc., can be written as superscript, but don't have to be. Show them both versions. Row 6 should be straightforward.

Answers

1 one / two / **three** / four / **five** / six / seven / **eight** / nine / ten
2 **first** / second / third / **fourth** / **fifth** / sixth / **seventh** / eighth / ninth / **tenth**
3 one / **two** / five / seven / nine / **eleven** / thirteen / **fifteen**
4 two / four / **six** / eight / ten / **twelve** / **fourteen** / sixteen

5 1st / **2nd** / 3rd / 4th / **5th** / 6th / **7th** / 8th / **9th** / 10th / **11th** / 12th
6 ten / **twenty** / thirty / forty / **fifty** / sixty / seventy / **eighty** / ninety

Exercise 7: Read, then listen and circle the words you hear

Use this exercise as the Closure. Exploit the visuals; ask where the photo was taken. Then ask students to read the notice in the photo. Finally, ask students to read the floor plan on the left. Now, students do the exercise. Ask them to read every word, allowing enough time for this. Play the CD once. Students circle the words they hear. Using an OHT/IWB, read out and point to each word, asking the students to say *yes* if they heard it, or *no* if they didn't hear it. Confirm right answers. If it emerges during this that there is significant disagreement, play the CD again, circling the words on the OHT/ IWB.

Answers

> **Transcript** 🔊 5.24 (0 mins, 52 secs)
>
> **1**
> A: Is there a coffee shop?
> B: Yes, it's on the first floor.
> A: Thank you.
>
> **2**
> A: Is there a cashpoint?
> B: Yes. It's on the tenth floor.
> A: Thank you.
>
> **3**
> A: Is this the fifth floor?
> B: Yes, this is the fifth floor. Men's clothes.
> A: OK. Thank you.
>
> **4**
> A: Where is the make-up?
> B: Make-up?
> A: Yes, make-up … cosmetics.
> B: On the second floor.

Lift	
maximum twelve persons	
(floors)	
⑩ (tenth)	bank, (cashpoint)
⑨ ninth	book shop
⑧ eighth	TVs, DVDs, CDs
❼ seventh	tables, chairs
❻ sixth	cups, plates
❺ (fifth)	(men)
❹ fourth	boys and girls, toys
❸ third	ladies
❷ (second)	perfume, (make-up)
❶ (first)	(coffee shop)
⓪ ground	supermarket
⬆ UP	⬇ DOWN

Closure

Use Exercise 7 as the Closure.

50 · S T R · S P R · S C R

Objectives

By the end of the lesson, students should be able to:

- read and say the consonant clusters *str, spr* and *scr* (without inserting a vowel sound between each consonant);
- read and say *ex* as /eks/;
- read and recognize spellings previously learnt.

Adaptations

Faster/mixed-ability classes	Directed self-study
Start with the words in Exercise 4 as a test of pronunciation and reading. On the basis of this, either start at Exercise 3 or go right back to the beginning of Exercise 1.	Use the words in Exercise 4 to check the students' recognition of the consonant clusters in the unit. Tell student(s) which exercises to do. If Exercise 1 is not necessary, begin at Exercise 2. Remind them that they can replay the CD, or pause it, if they wish.

Notes on new sounds

Some learners may put a vowel between each consonant in these clusters, e.g., *suturaight* for *straight*.

Words for revision
(also available as flashcards)

bun	eighth	eighty	eleventh	fifth	fifty
first	forty	fourth	fun	gun	ninety
ninth	one	rum	second	seventh	seventy
sixth	sixty	son	sun	tenth	third
thirteenth	thirty	to	twelfth	twenty	two
won					

New letters/words for this lesson
(also available as flashcards)

str /str/   spr /spr/   scr /skr/   x /eks/

astra	explain	express	extra	extreme	scrap
scrape	scream	screen	screw	screwdriver	script
scroll	scruffy	scrum	sprain	sprat	spray
spring	sprite	sprout	sprung	spry	straight
strain	strap	stray	stream	street	strife
strike	striker	string	strip	stripe	stroll
strong	struck	struggle	strum		

Introduction

This unit covers three consonant clusters composed of three elements. Some learners may find it difficult to pronounce these clusters without inserting a vowel between each consonant.

Write selected words from the revision list on the board/IWB (or use flashcards or an OHT). Choose between these activities:
- **students listen and repeat selected words**
- **designated students read out words**

Exercise 1: Read and say

Note that the words are carefully grouped. In section one, the target clusters are highlighted in red.
- Section one establishes the pronunciation of the target clusters.
- Section two practises the pronunciation of *str*.
- Section three practises the pronunciation of *spr*.
- Section four practises the pronunciation of *scr*.
- Section five mixes all the elements from the previous sections.

Discourage students from inserting a vowel between each consonant in the consonant clusters. The realization of *ex* as /eks/ is dealt with in Exercise 5, where it is combined with the target clusters of the unit.

Exploit the visual. Play the CD section by section. Students repeat after the CD.

Transcript 🔊 5.25 (2 mins, 32 secs)

1 s **2** say **3** st **4** stay **5** str **6** stray **7** s
8 sing **9** sp **10** spin **11** spr **12** spring **13** s
14 see **15** sc **16** scan **17** scr **18** screen

1 strap **2** stray **3** strain **4** straight **5** street
6 stream **7** strip **8** stripe **9** strife **10** strike
11 striker **12** string **13** stroll **14** strong **15** strum
16 struck **17** struggle **18** astra

1 sprat **2** spray **3** sprain **4** spring **5** sprite
6 sprout **7** sprung **8** spry

1 scrap **2** scrape **3** scream **4** screen **5** screw
6 script **7** scroll **8** scrum **9** scruffy

1 stray **2** spray **3** spring **4** string **5** screw
6 street **7** screen **8** strong **9** scroll **10** straight

Exercise 2: Listen and tick

Follow the usual procedure.

Answers

rain	train	stream	string	trip	struck	strike
scream	seem	screw	pry	pray	stray	street

Exercise 3: Trace and write

Follow the usual procedure. Monitor as the students work.

Exercise 4: Read and label

Follow the usual procedure.

Answers

1 screen   **2** spring   **3** screwdriver   **4** string   **5** strap

Exercise 5: Read, say and check

For the first time, a new element (*ex* /eks/ in row 1) is introduced in this type of exercise. As this is an exercise in which students try to work out the correct pronunciation of the words, the introduction of *ex* at this point may not present any problems. If any problems do occur, these will be resolved at the listening and checking stage. The recommended procedure here is to start with section one and to establish how to read *ex* quickly, playing the CD for that section after the students have thought about it. Then follow the usual procedure for the second section.

1 ex   **2** extra   **3** extreme   **4** explain   **5** express

1 crew   **2** screw   **3** press   **4** express   **5** pray
6 spray   **7** seen   **8** screen   **9** skip   **10** rip   **11** script
12 song   **13** strong   **14** roll   **15** scroll   **16** eight
17 straight   **18** scrape   **19** pain   **20** rain   **21** sprain
22 cream   **23** seem   **24** scream   **25** striker
26 astra   **27** extra   **28** plain   **29** explain

Exercise 6: Read, then listen and check

Follow the usual procedure.

an express train	a striker
an express bus	an extra striker
a shuttle bus	South Street
an express shuttle bus	North Street
extra ice, please	
a Sprite, please	
a Sprite with extra ice, please	
scroll up the screen	

Exercise 7: Find and circle words from Unit 50

Use this exercise as the Closure. Exploit the visuals. In the picture of the bus, can they read/recognize L-O-N-D-O-N? (Do not focus on Poole or Bournemouth.) Ask students to read the names of the streets in the pictures. Students to work with a partner. Ask them to circle the words they identify. Allow a reasonable time for this. Then check each picture in turn.

Answers

Closure

Use Exercise 7 for the Closure.

~NGLE ~NDLE

Objectives

By the end of the lesson, students should be able to:

■ read and say the consonant clusters *~ngle*, *~ndle*, *~mble* and *~mple*.

Adaptations

Faster/mixed-ability classes	Directed self-study
Start with the words in Exercise 3 as a test of pronunciation and reading. On the basis of this, start with Exercise 2 for stronger students, or return to Exercise 1.	Use the words in Exercise 3 to check the students' recognition of the consonant clusters in the unit. Carefully preview Exercise 7, an exercise which has only been done once before. Check the understanding of *syllable*(s). Do a further example.

Tell student(s) which exercises to do. If Exercise 1 is not necessary, begin at Exercise 2. Remind them that they can replay the CD, or pause it, if they wish. |

Words for revision
(also available as flashcards)

astra	scrap	scrape	scream	screen	screw
script	scroll	sprain	sprat	spray	spring
sprite	sprout	sprung	spry	straight	strain
strap	stray	stream	street	strife	strike
striker	string	strip	stripe	stroll	strong
struck	struggle	strum			

New letters/words for this lesson
(also available as flashcards)

~ngle /ŋgl/	~ndle /ndl/	~mble /mbl/	~mple /mpl/

amble	ample	angle	bangle	bumble	bundle
bungle	candle	crumble	crumple	dimple	example
fondle	grumble	handle	jingle	jungle	pimple
ramble	rumble	sample	scramble	simple	single
spindle	strangle	thimble	trample	tremble	triangle

Introduction

This unit covers four consonant clusters composed of three sounds. The nasals may present some problems and the distinction between *b* and *p* may present another problem. Write selected words from the revision list on the board/IWB (or use flashcards or an OHT). Choose between these activities:

- **students listen and repeat selected words**
- **designated students read out words**

Exercise 1: Read and say

The words are carefully grouped. The first two occurrences of the target clusters are highlighted in red.

- Section one revises the second and third elements of the target clusters by using words previously encountered.
- Section two practises the pronunciation of *~ngle*.
- Section three practises the pronunciation of *~ndle*.
- Section four practises the pronunciation of *~mble*.
- Section five practises the pronunciation of *~mple*.

In section five, /eks/ changes to /ekz/ in *example*, i.e., when a vowel follows. Exploit the visual. Play the CD section by section. Students repeat after the CD.

Transcript 🔊 5.29 (2 mins, 8 secs)

1 giggle **2** cradle **3** needle **4** middle **5** wobble
6 bubble **7** ripple **8** cripple

1 bang **2** bangle **3** angle **4** strangle **5** jingle
6 single **7** bungle **8** jungle **9** try **10** triangle

1 can **2** canned **3** candle **4** hand **5** handle
6 spin **7** spindle **8** fond **9** fondle **10** bundle

1 ram **2** ramble **3** scramble **4** tremble **5** bumble
6 rumble **7** crumble **8** grumble **9** thimble
10 amble

1 amp **2** ample **3** sample **4** example **5** trample
6 dimple **7** pimple **8** simple **9** rumple
10 crumple

Exercise 2: Listen and tick

Follow the usual procedure.

Answers

Transcript ⊙ **5.30** (0 mins, 40 secs)

amble   angle   tremble   grumble   single   ramble
bundle

crumple   jungle   pimple   scramble   example
thimble   simple

Exercise 3: Trace and write

Follow the usual procedure.

Exercise 4: Read and label

Follow the usual procedure.

Answers

1 scrambled egg   **2** candles   **3** jungle   **4** example
5 a bundle

Exercise 5: Listen, write in *ngle / ndle / mble / mple*

This is a new exercise type. Treat it as a modified dictation. Play the CD for the whole exercise while students follow in their books. Play each word separately while students write down their answers. Play the CD for the whole exercise again. Ask students to volunteer the right answers. When a right answer is volunteered, ask the student to spell it, to revise the names of letters. Confirm by writing the answer on the board.

Answers

Transcript ⊙ **5.31** (0 mins, 50 secs)

1 tri**angle**   **2** can**dle**   **3** tre**mble**   **4** exa**mple**
5 bun**dle**   **6** si**mple**   **7** si**ngle**   **8** gru**mble**   **9** ju**ngle**
10 sa**mple**

Exercise 6: Find and circle words you know, then listen and check

This can be broken down into two phases. Students work with a partner to find the words they know, then circle them. Then they change partners and compare answers, reading them to each other. For the second phase, ask the whole class about the new words (e.g., *speech bubble*).

Transcript ⊙ **5.32** (0 mins, 39 secs)

Draw and paint program   draw shapes   triangle
square   cube   circle   line   curve   angle   star
speech bubble

Exercise 7: Mark the syllables, then listen and check

This is a similar activity to Exercise 6 in Unit 43, except it contains listening as well. Check the understanding of *syllable*(s). Go through the example *birthday* and then do a further example. Students work individually and then compare their ideas with a partner. Allow a reasonable time for this. Then play the CD.

Answers

Transcript ⊙ **5.33** (1 min, 15 secs)

birth • day   birthday   can • dles   candles   bum • ble
bee   bumble bee   scram • bled egg   scrambled egg
tri • an • gle   triangle   sam • ple a song   sample a song
CD sin • gle   CD single   ex • am • ple   example
sim • ple   simple   app • le crum • ble   apple crumble
right an • gle   right angle   jun • gle drums   jungle
drums

Closure

Ask students to learn these words from Exercise 7 before beginning the next unit: *angle, apple, birthday, egg, example, sample, simple* and *single*.

52 ~ G E G E ~

Objectives

By the end of the lesson, students should be able to:

- associate and read *g* as /ʤ/ before *e, y* and *i* in words of one or more syllables.

Adaptations

Faster/mixed-ability classes	Directed self-study
Start with the words in Exercise 3 as a test of pronunciation and reading. On the basis of this, go to Exercise 2 for stronger students or return to Exercise 1.	Use the words in Exercise 3 to check the students' recognition of the consonant clusters in the unit. Tell student(s) which exercises to do. If Exercise 1 is not necessary, begin at Exercise 2. Remind them that they can replay the CD, or pause it, if they wish.

Notes on new sounds

Written *g* has two possible sounds: /g/ (the so-called *hard g* as in *rag*) and /ʤ/ (the so-called *soft g* as in *rage*). The soft *g* sounds the same as the letter *j*; they cannot be interchanged. The so-called soft *g* voiced affricate will cause problems for those native speakers of languages (and there are many) that either lack affricates completely or only have the unvoiced *ch*. Note that soft/hard *g* is less predictable than soft/hard *c*.

Words for revision
(also available as flashcards)

amble	ample	angle	bangle	bumble	bundle
bungle	candle	crumble	crumple	dimple	example
fondle	grumble	handle	jingle	jungle	pimple
ramble	rumble	sample	scramble	simple	single
spindle	strangle	thimble	trample	tremble	triangle

New letters/words for this lesson
(also available as flashcards)

~ge /ʤ/   ge~ /ʤ/

advantage	age	agency	agent	baggage
budge	cage	Egypt	gem	gene
general	gent	gentle	germ	German
Germany	gin	gym	gypsum	huge
image	page	passengers	rage	sage
stage	stooge	surgery	village	wage

Introduction

This unit completes the coverage of the *soft g* voiced affricate /ʤ/. As mentioned earlier, the frequent lack of this sound in other languages may cause difficulties. These difficulties will affect pronunciation and writing more than reading perhaps, but it is worth pointing out as an issue and giving the students some practice.

Write selected words from the revision list on the board/IWB (or use flashcards or an OHT). Choose between these activities:

- students listen and repeat selected words
- designated students read out words

Exercise 1: Read and say

The words are carefully grouped.

- Sections one and two contrast the reading of *g* and *ge* at the end of a syllable.
- Sections three and four practise the pronunciation of *ge~*.
- Section five revises initial *j* and practises the pronunciation of syllables beginning *gy*.

~age is pronounced /ɪʤ/ when at the end of a word of more than one syllable. Exploit the visual. Play the CD section by section. Students repeat after the CD. Ask students to find the names and nationalities in the last three sections.

Transcript 🔊 5.34 (2 mins, 38 secs)

1 rag **2** rage **3** wag **4** wage **5** stag **6** stage
7 ace **8** pace **9** age **10** page **11** race **12** rage

1 age **2** cage **3** page **4** rage **5** sage **6** stage
7 wage **8** hug **9** huge **10** get **11** gent
12 ginger

1 gel **2** gent **3** germ **4** German **5** Germany
6 gem **7** gene **8** general **10** gentle

1 agent **2** agency **3** image **4** village **5** gym
6 gypsum **7** Egypt **8** surgery **9** advantage

1 Jim **2** gym **3** Jem **4** gem **5** jingle **6** gin
7 ginger **8** Jenny **9** general **10** wage **11** stage
12 gent **13** agent **14** image **15** huge **16** gene
17 gym **18** Egypt **19** page **20** age **21** surgery

Exercise 2: Listen and tick

Follow the usual procedure.

Answers

stage	rag	wage	image	gent	stool	Jane
agency	Egypt	age	gram	huge	bug	gene

Exercise 3: Trace and write

Students should not attempt to copy the printed *g* shape. They should follow the handwritten shape given. Although *g* can be written in other ways, this need not be focused on. Follow the usual procedure.

Exercise 4: Read and label

Follow the usual procedure.

Answers

1 gym **2** Egypt **3** Germany **4** pages **5** cage

Exercise 5: Find and circle the Gs, then put these words in the box with the same *g* sound

Use this exercise as the Closure. This is a new exercise type; treat it as a modified dictation. Exploit the visual and explain these are all airport-related words. Point out that all the labels are in capital letters. Play the CD for the whole exercise while students follow in their books. Play each phrase separately while students write down their answers, preferably using lower-case letters as well as the correct handwritten form of *g*. Play the CD for the whole exercise again. Ask students to volunteer the right answers. When a right answer is volunteered, ask the student to spell it, to revise the names of letters. Confirm by writing the answer on the board.

Answers

g in *got*	ba**gg**age, under**g**round, **g**reen
g in *gel*	bagga**g**e, passen**g**ers, a**g**ency, **g**ents, villa**g**e
g in *sing*	meetin**g**, shoppin**g**

Exercise 6: Read, then listen and check

Follow the usual procedure.

Answers

1 get **2** gem **3** jet **4** gym **5** Jenny **6** German
7 huge **8** hugging **9** surgery **10** cage **11** stag
12 stagger **13** stage **14** general **15** gel **16** pace
17 pack **18** pain **19** page **20** rage **21** bag
22 age **23** baggage

a village in Germany	travel agency
going to Egypt	car rental agency
baggage claim	germs in the surgery

excess baggage
air passengers
underground train

Closure

Use Exercise 6 as the Closure.

53 · O OU OW

Objectives

By the end of the lesson, students should be able to:

- read final *ow* as /aʊ/ (as in *cow*), except after *bl, cr, fl, gl, gr, sh, sl, sn, st* and *thr*, when it is /əʊ/;
- read final *o* in *radio* and *woe*, and single *o* before a single consonant (as in *Microsoft*) as /əʊ/;
- read *ou* as /aʊ/ (revision from Unit 34);
- read *oo* as /uː/ (revision from Unit 16);
- read other spellings from previous units.

Adaptations

Faster/mixed-ability classes	Directed self-study
Start with the words in Exercise 1, section five as a test of pronunciation and reading for the unit. On the basis of this, go to Exercise 2 for stronger students, or begin with Exercise 1.	Use the words in Exercise 3 to check the students' recognition of the spellings in the unit. Tell student(s) which exercises to do. If Exercise 1 is not necessary, begin at Exercise 2. Remind them that they can replay the CD, or pause it, if they wish.

Words for revision
(also available as flashcards)

advantage	age	agency	agent	baggage
budge	cage	Egypt	gem	gene
general	gent	gentle	germ	German
Germany	gin	gym	gypsum	huge
image	page	passengers	rage	sage
stage	stooge	surgery	village	wage

Sound variants of spelling already encountered (also available as flashcards)

o /əʊ/	ou /aʊ/	ow /əʊ/			
blow	blown	close	Coca-Cola	crow	flow
flown	glow	grow	grown	low	Microsoft
o'clock	Oh!	OK	open	pillow	post
radio	show	slow	slower	snow	solo
throw	thrown	toe	video	willow	window
woe	yellow				

Introduction

The spelling patterns in this unit determine the vowel. Students will need to be able to discriminate between the two pronunciations of *ow*.

- **In words beginning with one consonant or *br, pr, tr* + *ow*, such as *cow* or *brow*, the vowel is /aʊ/.**
- **In single-syllable words beginning *fl* or *sl*, or two-syllable words with the stress on the first syllable as in *window*, *ow* is /əʊ/.**
- **Where the stress falls on the last syllable, e.g., *allow* and *endow*, the vowel is /aʊ/, but this is not part of the unit.**

Write selected words from the revision list on the board/IWB (or use flashcards or an OHT). Choose between these activities:

- **students listen and repeat selected words**
- **designated students read out words**

Exercise 1: Read and say

This quite a difficult exercise, as the notes on pronunciation in the Introduction would suggest. However, do not try to teach the rules in the Introduction. Few native readers could articulate them, but they can read *ow* in different contexts perfectly competently. It is a question of familiarity, which is what this exercise and all the others go some way to establishing. In light of this, take the exercise slowly and carefully, repeating a section if necessary.

- Section one revises previously encountered spellings of /aʊ/ and contains two examples of the triphthong /aʊə/ (*our, ours*).
- Section two mixes *ow* as in *now*, and *ow* as in *grow*, and also covers /əʊ/ as in *toe* or *no*.
- Section three is confined to /əʊ/, as in *flow, yellow*.
- Section four practises previously encountered spellings and new spellings of /əʊ/.
- Section five revises elements from the first four sections.

Exploit the visual, which contains *ow* representing two different vowels. Play the CD section by section. Students repeat after the CD.

Transcript 🔊 5.37 (3 mins, 27 secs)

1 how   2 now   3 cow   4 down   5 town   6 brown
7 frown   8 tower   9 flower   10 shower   11 out
12 our   13 ours

1 now   2 out   3 no   4 road   5 toe   6 open
7 home   8 low   9 slow   10 grow

1 low   2 blow   3 crow   4 grow   5 grown   6 show
7 slow   8 slower   9 throw   10 flow   11 flown
12 glow   13 pillow   14 window   15 yellow
16 willow

1 no   2 so   3 go   4 coat   5 woe   6 note   7 vote
8 zone   9 smoke   10 smoking   11 close   12 closed
13 OK   14 open   15 hotel   16 solo   17 video
18 radio   19 Coca-Cola   20 post   21 o'clock
22 Microsoft

1 now   2 slow   3 snow   4 show   5 how   6 shower
7 grow   8 grown   9 glow   10 throw   11 thrown
12 OK   13 Oh!   14 open   15 closed   16 window
17 down   18 solo   19 radio   20 our   21 boat
22 coat   23 out   24 so   25 ours   26 town

Exercise 2: Listen and tick

Follow the usual procedure.

Answers

Transcript 🔊 5.38 (0 mins, 41 secs)

now   road   brown   it's snow   our   open   slow
thrown   window   flower   yellow   show her
glow   frown

Exercise 3: Trace and write

Follow the usual procedure.

Exercise 4: Read and label

Follow the usual procedure.

Answers

1 black   2 brown   3 green   4 blue   5 yellow   6 red

Exercise 5: Find the sounds

Use this as the Closure. The answers should be completed on the board. Write the categories on the board/IWB (or OHT), as they appear in the table. Read the words given as examples in the table. Get students to read out each notice. Ask them which words should go in which column, and write the word(s) in the right column.

Answers

o in *vote, boat*	road closed, post, yellow, old, no smoking, slow, hotel, windows, closed
o in *got, not*	office
o in *cow*	out

Exercise 6: Read, then listen and check

Follow the usual procedure.

Transcript 🔊 5.39 (1 min, 37 secs)

1 now   2 no   3 note   4 boat   5 so   6 slow
7 shower   8 how   9 our   10 yell   11 yellow
12 pill   13 pillow   14 post   15 o'clock   16 OK
17 out   18 go

out of town   closed, open at ten
no smoking   Post Office
road closed   Bay Hotel
Yellow Pages   outdoor pool

Radio One
Microsoft Windows
slow down
down and out

Closure

Use Exercise 5 as the Closure, as suggested above.

54   P H ~ G H

Objectives

By the end of the lesson, students should be able to:

- read and say the letters *ph* as /f/;
- read and say *gh* as /f/ when not followed by *t*;
- read and say *laugh, cough, rough, tough* and *enough* with the correct vowels;
- read other spellings from previous units.

Adaptations

Faster/mixed-ability classes	Directed self-study
Start with the words in Exercise 3 as a test of pronunciation and reading. On the basis of this, go to Exercise 2 for stronger students, or begin with Exercise 1.	Use the words in Exercise 3 to check the students' recognition of the spellings in the unit. Tell student(s) which exercises to do. If Exercise 1 is not necessary, begin at Exercise 2. Remind them that they can replay the CD, or pause it, if they wish.

Words for revision
(also available as flashcards)

blow	blown	close	Coca-Cola	crow	flow
flown	glow	grow	grown	low	Microsoft
o'clock	Oh!	OK	open	pillow	post
radio	show	slow	slower	snow	solo
throw	thrown	toe	video	willow	window
woe	yellow				

Sound variants of a spelling already encountered (also available as flashcards)

ph /f/   ~gh /f/

alpha	alphabet	cough	enough	graph
laugh	nephew	phantom	pharmacy	Philip
phone	phono	photo	photocopy	phrase
physical	physics	rough	sphere	telephone
tough	typhoid			

Introduction

The spellings covered in this unit focus on *ph* and *gh* as realizations of /f/. Write selected words from the revision list on the board/IWB (or use flashcards or an OHT). Choose between these activities:

- **students listen and repeat selected words**
- **designated students read out words**

Exercise 1: Read and say

- Section one revises previously learnt spellings of *f* as well as /ɒ/, /ɪ/ and /əʊ/ which are related to their representation in words with *ph*.
- Sections two and three focus on *ph*.
- Section four focuses on words ending in *gh*.
- Section five mixes the elements from the first four sections.

Exploit the visual. Ask students if they can see a name anywhere in the exercise (*Philip* in section two). Play the CD section by section. Students repeat after the CD.

Transcript ⊙ 5.40 (1 min, 55 secs)

1 fox   **2** foam   **3** fin   **4** fine   **5** bone   **6** phone
7 photo

1 phone   **2** telephone   **3** photo   **4** phono   **5** phrase
6 physics   **7** physical   **8** phantom   **9** pharmacy
10 Philip   **11** photocopy

1 alpha   **2** alphabet   **3** sphere   **4** graph
5 photograph   **6** nephew   **7** typhoid

1 laugh   **2** cough   **3** rough   **4** tough   **5** enough

1 phone   **2** alphabet   **3** photo   **4** graph   **5** nephew
6 rough   **7** physics   **8** tough   **9** pharmacy
10 cough   **11** photograph

Exercise 2: Listen and tick

Follow the usual procedure.

Answers

Transcript ⊙ 5.41 (0 mins, 41 secs)

photo	phone	raise	foam	phone	sphere
graph					

rough	coffee	lark	tough	graph	a few
enough					

Exercise 3: Trace and write

Follow the usual procedure. Monitor and correct, as several ascenders and descenders are involved here.

Exercise 4: Read and label

Follow the usual procedure.

Answers

1 photo   **2** graph   **3** alphabet   **4** sphere   **5** phantom

Exercise 5: Read, say and check

For the first section of this exercise, follow the usual procedure. The words in the second section are arranged in rows by the vowel they contain. This helps students practise associating the possible different representations of a given vowel. Get the students to identify the target vowel of a row by reading the first word. Practise it aloud for each row. Students can then read the remainder of the row to a partner.

1 graph   **2** laugh   **3** off   **4** cough   **5** tough   **6** stuff
7 alpha   **8** alphabet   **9** foot   **10** photo   **11** foam
12 phone   **13** few   **14** nephew   **15** boy   **16** foil
17 try   **18** typhoid   **19** queer   **20** spear   **21** here
22 sphere   **23** fizz   **24** physics

or   for   your   ought   born
now   how   our   ours   pound   count   down
no   go   so   slow   phone   photo   o'clock   OK
good   wood   could   should   would
not   off   soft   cough

Exercise 6: Find and circle words from Units 51–54, then listen and check

Follow the usual procedure.

Answers

3G   My **Phone** Touch Screen   **radio** streaming   **phone**
phone book   text messages   **video**   camera
photos & **images**   tools   web browser   **graph**
alphabet game   tunes & **samples**

Unit 51 ~NGLE ~NDLE ~MBLE ~MPLE: sample
Unit 52 ~GE GE~: image
Unit 53 O OU OW: radio, video
Unit 54 PH ~GH: phone (x3), photo, graph, alphabet

Exercise 7: Add the key words, then listen and check

Follow the usual procedure.

a able about all am an and & at @ **be** been birth bit born both but **can** come could count day did do doing don't down drink each eat English **enough** first for from get go going got had he her here Hi him how if I **in** it just let little lot may me mean might morning much **must** near nice night no not now o'clock OK on or **ought** our ours out phone photo please pound read room saw say see seen she shop should slow so some soon than **thank** that the them thing this too up us we well went we're when which **while** will with won't word would yes you your yours

Exercise 8: Dictation

Follow the usual procedure.

Answers

1 tough	T-O-U-G-H	tough
2 cough	C-O-U-G-H	cough
3 pharmacy	P-H-A-R-M-A-C-Y	pharmacy
4 physics	P-H-Y-S-I-C-S	physics
5 alpha	A-L-P-H-A	alpha

Closure

Learn the meaning and spelling of these useful words from Exercise 1 (it is possible students know them orally already):
- Row 2: words 1, 3, 5, 6
- Row 3: words 2, 5, 6
- Row 4: all the words

Read all the numbers first. Then confirm by putting the numbers on the board. If time allows, ask students to read out the words.

55 K N G N W R W H

Objectives
By the end of the lesson, students should be able to:

- recognize the combinations *kn, gn,* and *wr* as containing an initial silent letter;
- recognize and read when an initial *h* or *w* is silent.

Adaptations

Faster/mixed-ability classes	Directed self-study
Start with the words in Exercise 1, section five as a test of pronunciation and reading. On the basis of this, go to Exercise 2 for stronger students, or begin with Exercise 1.	Use the words in Exercise 1, section five to check the students' recognition of the spellings in the unit. Tell student(s) which exercises to do. If Exercise 1 is not necessary, begin at Exercise 2. Remind them that they can replay the CD, or pause it, if they wish.

Notes on new sounds
All these *silent* letters used to be pronounced, with the exception of the initial silent *h*, which is found in words borrowed from Romance languages.

Words for revision
(also available as flashcards)

alpha	alphabet	cough	enough	graph	laugh
nephew	phantom	pharmacy	Philip	phone	phono
photo	photocopy	phrase	physical	physics	rough
sphere	telephone	tough	typhoid		

Sound variants of spellings already encountered (also available as flashcards)

kn /n/   gn /n/   wr /r/   wh /h/

gnash	gnat	gnaw	honour	hour	knack
knee	knew	knickers	knife	knight	knit
knock	knot	know	knuckle	who	whole
whom	whose	Wrangler	wrap	wreck	wren
wrench	wring	wrinkle	wrist	write	writer
writing	wrong	wrote			

Introduction
The spellings covered in this unit focus on silent letters. See the note above for a brief explanation of why they are now silent, or always were. The initial consonant is no longer pronounced in the clusters *kn, gn* and *wr*. Initial *w* is not pronounced when *wh* is followed by /uː/ or /əʊ/.

Write selected words from the revision list on the board/IWB (or use flashcards or an OHT). Choose between these activities:

- students listen and repeat selected words
- designated students read out words

Exercise 1: Read and say

- Section one matches initial *n* with initial *kn* to establish they sound the same. *Gnat* is included as an example of the silent *g*.
- Section two introduces further examples of *kn* and *gn*.
- Section three introduces *wr*.
- Section four mixes examples of all the target letters.

Exploit the visual. Play the CD section by section. Students repeat after the CD.

Transcript 🔊 5.46 (2 mins, 38 secs)

1 not   2 knot   3 new   4 knew   5 no   6 know
7 Nat   8 gnat

1 knack   2 knee   3 knit   4 knife   5 knight
6 knickers   7 know   8 knew   9 knot   10 knock
11 knit   12 knuckle   13 gnat   14 gnash   15 gnaw

1 ring   2 wring   3 rap   4 wrap   5 right   6 write
7 wrangler   8 wren   9 wreck   10 wrong
11 wrinkle   12 writer   13 writing   14 wrote
15 wrench   16 wrist

1 our   2 hour   3 honour   4 do   5 who   6 whose
7 whom   8 hole   9 whole

1 knife   2 write   3 knit   4 gnat   5 wrap   6 knock
7 knee   8 knuckle   9 wrinkle   10 wrong   11 know
12 who   13 hour   14 whole   15 whose

Exercise 2: Listen and tick

Follow the usual procedure.

Answers

Transcript 🔊 5.47 (0 mins, 38 secs)

knock	wrong	know	knife	hour	whose	who
gnat	know	gnash	knew	knot	wring	writer

Exercise 3: Trace and write

Follow the usual procedure. Monitor and correct, as several ascenders and descenders are involved here.

Exercise 4: Read and label

Follow the usual procedure.

Answers

1 knife   **2** knee   **3** gnat   **4** wrist   **5** two hours

Exercise 5: Read, say and check

Follow the usual procedure.

Transcript 🔊 5.48 (1 min, 16 secs)

1 right   **2** write   **3** ring   **4** wring   **5** wrong   **6** nice
7 knife   **8** need   **9** knee   **10** ours   **11** hours
12 hoot   **13** whom   **14** blue   **15** screw   **16** do
17 who   **18** you   **19** whose   **20** pole   **21** whole
22 home   **23** know   **24** queue   **25** dew   **26** knew
27 not   **28** knot   **29** knock   **30** wrote   **31** wrangler
32 writing   **33** reading

Exercise 6: Read, then listen and check

Follow the usual procedure.

Answers

Transcript 🔊 5.49 (1 min, 7 secs)

night	write	right	might
hi	how	him	here	he	her	who	whose
no	not	now	near	nice	know	knew
read	room	wrong	write	wrote	right
I	know	how	to	read	and	write	now

Exercise 7: Listen and highlight the silent letters

This is best done as an individual activity, with partners checking each other's work when everyone has finished the exercise. Set a reasonable time limit for the exercise.

Transcript 🔊 5.50 (0 mins, 42 secs)

1 knife   **2** wrong   **3** whole   **4** gnaw   **5** gnash
6 knew   **7** knock   **8** wrote   **9** wrinkle   **10** when

Exercise 8: Tick (✓) the same sounds and cross (✗) the different sounds at the beginning of the words

Follow the usual procedure. Unlike previous versions of this exercise type where students looked for the same central vowel sounds, students here are looking for the same *initial* sounds.

Answers

1 ✓   **2** ✗   **3** ✗   **4** ✓   **5** ✓   **6** ✗   **7** ✓   **8** ✗   **9** ✓
10 ✗   **11** ✓   **12** ✓

Exercise 9: Find words from Unit 55

This is recommended as the Closure. Follow the usual procedure.

Answers

Z	W	R	E	C	K	J	U
W	R	A	P	K	N	E	E
R	I	W	G	N	O	W	H
I	T	R	N	I	W	H	O
S	E	O	A	F	I	O	U
T	M	N	W	E	N	S	R
D	Y	G	N	A	T	E	K
W	H	O	L	E	G	N	N

Closure

Use Exercise 9 as the Closure.

56 | E A | A I | E Y | E I R

Objectives
By the end of the lesson, students should be able to:

- recognize and read cases of the same spelling representing different vowels, e.g., *bean/bread, they/their, got/what* and *spire/liar/pyre*.

Adaptations

Faster/mixed-ability classes	Directed self-study
Start with the words in Exercise 1, section five as a test of pronunciation and reading. On the basis of this, go to Exercise 2 for stronger students, or begin with Exercise 1.	Use the words in Exercise 1, section five to check the students' recognition of the spellings in the unit. Tell student(s) which exercises to do. If Exercise 1 is not necessary, begin at Exercise 2. Remind them that they can replay the CD, or pause it, if they wish.

Words for revision
(also available as flashcards)

gnash	gnat	gnaw	honour	hour	knack	knee
knew	knickers	knife	knight	knit	knock	knot
know	knuckle	who	whole	whom	whose	Wrangler
wrap	wreck	wren	wrench	wring	wrinkle	wrist
write	writer	writing	wrong	wrote		

New letter sequence and alternative vowels for spellings already encountered
(also available as flashcards)

ea/ai /e/   ey /eɪ/   eir/are /eə/   ere /ɜː/
ire/iar/yre/yer/ier /aɪə/

bread	byre	dead	drier	flyer	grey	head
liar	pyre	said	their	they	tread	want
was	were	what				

Introduction
This unit focuses on special vowel spellings – spellings normally associated with other sounds. Write selected words from the revision list on the board/IWB (or use flashcards or an OHT). Choose between these activities:
- **students listen and repeat selected words**
- **designated students read out words**

Exercise 1: Read and say
This is a long exercise. If desired, break it after section five, do Exercise 3 and then return to section six.
- Section one revises spellings for vowels already encountered.
- Section two covers the spelling *ea* for the vowel (/e/), in *bread,* and shows that the same vowel is used for *e* in *bred.*
- Section three introduces instances of *ey* representing the sound which is usually spelt *ay*, e.g., *grey/say*.
- Section four covers instances of /ɒ/ being written as *a*, and /ɜː/ being spelt *ere*.

- Section five covers *yre/yer* in *pyre, dryer*, etc.
- Section 6 contains a mixture of the elements from the first five sections.

Exploit the visual (*bread*) as contrasting with the *ea* spellings in the first section. Play the CD section by section. Students repeat after the CD.

Transcript ⊙ 5.51 (2 mins, 55 secs)

1 be   **2** been   **3** bean   **4** each   **5** tea   **6** teach
7 teacher   **8** team   **9** cheap   **10** stream   **11** pay
12 paid   **13** made

1 bed   **2** bred   **3** bread   **4** head   **5** dead   **6** tread
7 said

1 may   **2** say   **3** they   **4** grey   **5** air   **6** share
7 their   **8** there

1 hot   **2** knot   **3** what   **4** was   **5** want   **6** her
7 hers   **8** fur   **9** girl   **10** were   **11** car   **12** far
13 are

1 fire   **2** wire   **3** spire   **4** shire   **5** dire   **6** flyer
7 pyre   **8** byre   **9** dryer   **10** drier   **11** liar

1 beach   **2** bread   **3** heel   **4** heap   **5** head   **6** way
7 laid   **8** said   **9** say   **10** deal   **11** dead   **12** hay
13 grey   **14** pray   **15** they   **16** fair   **17** dare
18 their   **19** here   **20** were   **21** there   **22** are

Exercise 2: Listen and tick
Follow the usual procedure.

Answers

Transcript ⊙ 5.52 (0 mins, 38 secs)

what	their	said	may	there	her	our
fire	why	fire	dead	bread	fly	grey

Exercise 3: Trace and write

Follow the usual procedure. Monitor and correct, as several ascenders are involved here.

Exercise 4: Read and label

Follow the usual procedure.

Answers

1 hairdryer **2** fire **3** grey hair **4** wire-cutters
5 head

Exercise 5: Read, then listen and check

Follow the usual procedure.

> **Transcript** 5.53 (1 min, 7 secs)
>
> **1** I **2** you **3** he **4** she **5** we **6** they **7** me
> **8** him **9** her **10** them **11** are **12** was **13** were
> **14** who **15** what **16** which **17** whose **18** when
> **19** why **20** want **21** said **22** here **23** there
> **24** our **25** their **26** right **27** wrong **28** bread

Exercise 6: Match the words in the box with words with the same sound, then listen and check

Students work individually, reading the words in the grey box aloud in order to match them with the words in the table. Then they compare answers with a partner. Elicit the word pairs from the students and confirm or correct.

Answers

> **Transcript** 5.54 (1 min, 15 secs)
>
> tell – smell   we – she   here – dear   who – do
> are – bar   were – her   how – now   mile – while
>
> beach – teach   said – head   would – could
> might – light   slow – know   why – sky   hat – that
> ten – when
>
> town – down   what – got   grey – they   there – their
> June – soon   drawn – born   kiss – this   tin – spin

Exercise 7: Add the key words, then listen and check

Follow the usual procedure.

Answers

> **Transcript** 5.55 (2 mins, 42 secs)
>
> a **able** about all am an and & are at @ be been birth bit born both but can come **could** count day did do doing don't down drink each eat English enough first for from get go going good got had he **her** here Hi him hour how I if in it just know let little lot may me mean might morning much must near nice night no not now o'clock OK on or ought our ours out phone photo **please** pound read room said saw say see seen she shop should slow so some **soon** than thank that the their them there they thing this too up us want was we well went were we're what **when** which while who whose will with won't word would write wrong yes you your

Closure

Use the pictures on the right of Exercise 6 for the Closure. Working with a partner, students read the notices to each other. Monitor. Finally, tell students they can now read the top 100 words in English and many new words as they meet them.

Handwriting paper